OWN YOUR
PURPOSE
& REALIZE YOUR
POTENTIAL

OWN YOUR
PURPOSE
& REALIZE YOUR
POTENTIAL

EXPERTS RECOUNT THEIR ADVENTURES TO SUCCESS

LESLIE THOMAS FLOWERS

OWN YOUR PURPOSE & REALIZE YOUR POTENTIAL
Experts Recount their Adventures to Success

CONTRIBUTING AUTHORS

Donna Brown

Aimee Chandler

Jeanette Chasworth

Megan Davies

Esha Herbert-Davis

Leslie Flowers

Gillian Fountain

Katie Gailes

Haley Gray

Chrystal Harris

Aigars Kauliņš

Sheyenne Kreamer

Olga Monroe

Ashley Morrison

Deborah Oronzio

Divya Parekh

Judy Prokopiak

Marie Snider

Lyndah Tello

Krysti Turznik

Susan Walsh

Julie Ward

TABLE OF CONTENTS

ACKNOWLEDGEMENTS

To MY TWO children Michelle and Matthew, my grandchildren Brooke, Sydney, Julia and Blake, for loving me unconditionally.

To my friend of ten years, J. Ross Cornwell, first editor of the Napoleon Hill Foundation newsletter and editor of the most celebrated versions of *Think and Grow Rich* by Napoleon Hill studied today. Through ups and downs, Ross stood by my side as a true friend.

To the heart centered authors herein who knew there were those already waiting for their message and stepped out to share it now, rather than someday, maybe.

To Coach Divya Parekh for her partnership in publishing and to her team for fulfilling this book in both digital and print format.

To my clients who allow me to share in the joy of their constant and consistent successes over time. It is my greatest privilege to walk by your side.

Thank you.

Leslie Flowers

PREFACE

IT IS A privilege and an honor both to know Leslie Flowers and to introduce her and her work to you. She is a trailblazing woman of great wisdom, strength, perseverance and integrity. And she is so very committed to transforming people's lives and businesses: she is truly a performance catalyst.

I first had the pleasure of meeting Leslie over a decade ago. At that time, she organized and conducted monthly mastermind meetings to teach and discuss principles of success and I had the good fortune of attending one of her events. I found her to be an extraordinarily dedicated woman with whom I shared mutual passions on many levels and we soon became fast friends.

Leslie is amazing in her steadfast devotion and commitment to her craft. She has culled and taught the most important aspects of *Think and Grow Rich* (and other great works including her own bestselling book *Champion: 21st Century Women: Guardians of Wealth and Legacy*) for over 14,000 hours. Ten years in, she continues to conduct ongoing in-depth trainings in how to be successful in life and business. That is mastery!

So it is no surprise (although it is a delight) that Leslie had the brilliant idea to gather a group of thought leaders and achievers and ask them to identify for others how they arrived at their purpose: how it came to be that they arrived at doing their life's work, their first steps, and how they tapped into their infinite potential.

Leslie has overcome some great obstacles and turned them into gold bricks to pave the road for herself and others that come after her. And that is what she set out to do here with this anthology. She will share her story here and others will recount their adventures to success, revealing previously untold messages that will inform, entertain and instruct you in your next steps to take to be successful in living your purpose.

This is an anthology you will want to refer to again and again and share with those you love and care about.

To your unstoppable success in living your true purpose.

Blessings,

Susan Walsh
SusanWalsh.com
Founder, Unprecedented Lives

INTRODUCTION

IN LATE 2006, still working in Corporate America for forty years and with ten years of personal development and leadership training under my belt, the book The Secret took the world unexpectedly, by storm.

I started a monthly Meetup group called "The Secret Society" with the purpose of studying the practices and practitioners in the film. The movie was released in late 2007. The meetings were filled with people hungry for anything about the Law of Attraction. I loved the energy and excitement I felt facilitating the group. I remember wondering how I might turn this sideline into a real job.

That is when, through a few unusual circumstances, I landed on a website with a picture of the grandfatherly narrator of the movie, Bob Proctor. Not unusual for me, almost guided without realizing, I bought a business in a box and went to learn from Proctor and his team. Their specialty? Think and Grow Rich by Napoleon Hill. I had never heard of it.

Since early 2008 when I began teaching the principles in this classic, until today, I have never stopped studying and teaching this work... not for one day. I didn't stop to consider why I loved this work so much and in the next five years, I had facilitated some twenty-five masterminds.

In 2013 when I learned about the gender wage gap, my Why came through an Awakening. This material was exactly what women needed to ask for what they deserve and be paid, and, they did not have one clue about the concepts.

In the moment when I heard the date 2054 as the point of the close of the wage gap, I became aware of chills, whispers, warmth in my heart and the answer became clear. I had already accrued some 7000 hours of teaching and facilitating masterminds and was One woman that could teach women these concepts!

At the time of publishing this book, my high-performance women's mastermind was in its twenty-first consecutive business quarter with consistent extraordinary results for those willing to stay the course and willing to do the work. Willing.

I was willing to go heads down and do the work. I maintained it applying for myself twenty years of training, topped off with the most vital and actionable material to yield success; for my students and me.

What I learned from my clients over ten years through practice, trial and error is that it is the seed of a very clear and definite purpose that fuels the desire to have success manifest. That is, to hold what they dreamed of 'in their hands.' And that it is that desire that has us overcome any and all obstacles, being persistent, that allows us to realize that what we want is already moving toward us at the same vibration or velocity we are moving toward it.

I saw that my clients were experiencing extraordinary results every quarter and with consistency.

In 2016 I created a live event for women small business owners and entrepreneurs along with my mastermind clients, to feed them what they needed to dream, build and achieve businesses they loved. Another event in 2017 was about impact, influence, and income.

In 2018 the theme became Awakening Your Infinite Potential, and I hosted a global online telesummit with two dozen coaches, discussing one or two specific awakening moments and their very first steps into action.

It was about intuitive moments, hunches, nudges from the universe, how to recognize them and almost more importantly, what were their first two steps toward realizing that idea. I learned that ideas are gifts that circulate about the universe and it's those few who get the idea and hold it tightly, make it clear and fall in love with it could be lost in an instant by confusion. When we get a new idea, we don't know what to do next, and that can douse the flame of desire.

Because I know we learn best in small bites and review with consistency in spaced intervals over time, having twenty-six different stories would be a gold mine. Twenty-six different awakenings, each with exact steps to take next. Hosting most of those interview in two days gave me a significant private transformation for myself. And it would work for others.

During the telesummit, I got the 'idea,' with the approval of the presenters, to transcribe their awakenings and next steps and create this book for those who want to quickly recognize ideas, awakening, nudges given to us and exactly what to do to perpetuate the desire required to 'bring the idea home.'

Like a dozen times before, I had an idea in an instant and 'moved out on it.' Fast action is a requirement, and here we are.

For Whom This Book is Written

This book is written for the woman (or man) who are already on their way to greatness. You've had a taste of it already. You are already a success. You are already confident.

You will have a good idea if this book is right for you if you know you are already on your path yet are clear there is more to know. More to reshape the "fire, aim, ready" mindset to change it to one of "ready, aim, then fire." You know that's more effective.

You are looking for your next step to expand your success, to grow your business further, to predict financial outcomes with regularity, to source and embrace momentum ... because of one thing that is likely the thing that brings you to tears ... your Legacy. What will you leave behind? What will be written about you after you are gone?

You know your purpose and have a message you want to get out in the world in a 'big way.'

You are clear that learning has a direct impact on earnings. You've proven that yourself so you are always pursuing new ways of thinking and doing. You know you have a purpose that will serve mankind, and you are on fire to share it.

You have had life-altering awakenings already, some monstrous, and come through them with flair. Never mind how long it may have taken you. In fact, it's primarily for you if you know instinctively by now that for every down there is a matching 'up' and you are in a place of 'expecting' the 'up' to show up almost any day. And while you may be impatient, you still keep walking. You are ready to quickly recognize an awakening and get into immediate action toward it.

You are open to adding new information to your tool belt of skills and are intentional about finding your purpose and realizing your potential.

You are a no-nonsense, do-it-yourself (for the most part), get it done person. You can do nearly anything ... with directions.

This book is for you, right now, if ... you see yourself in all or part of the description above.

Now YOU are ready to awaken your own infinite potential.

For Whom This Book is Not Written

This book is not for you if you bristled at all or part of the description of who this book is for. It's foreign to you. You don't see yourself this way. Not right now. You could be somewhere in between of course. You get to decide if you are close to taking this on 'now,' or not now.

This book is not for you if you don't believe you have greatness within you. You don't believe you can succeed and you have proof from past failures.

You are sure that people, conditions, and circumstances are responsible for your lot in life -- particularly your inability to be the success you dream of being. You have not yet accepted full responsibility for all of your life ... the way it is, and the way it is not.

If you decide this book is not for you right now because you match all or some of the attributes I've just mentioned, it's all right. Our 'inner journey' is just that ... our own, and it takes time. Creating from an awakening is a process. Not being ready now only means that you will certainly be ready at some point.

If you are looking for things you disagree with, that you are sure don't work (you've tried them before) and are unwilling to believe that there is a way to expand your business, get your message out, and leave a Legacy, you are not ready for this book right now.

What I know for sure is this: You will know when you possess the mindset that is ready for this book because yours matches the description for whom this book is written.

How To Use This Book

The information in this book is not to 'replace' what you already know. It is to 'add to' what you know to develop a solid foundation of faith. Faith in yourself and faith in the 'way of the universe.'

Read a chapter and pause for a moment to check in to see if the information resonates. Think about a similar awakening and chart your first two steps.

Because we are never given an idea we cannot do, note ideas you get along the way. If any word used musters up an unpleasant feeling in your midsection, this is a good thing. Pause for a moment and jot down what it was. When you revisit it at another time, look to see where this 'trigger' came from. Was it an incident? Do you remember your age?

Earmark a certain amount of time for reading. Do only that. Mixing reading with other activities will interrupt the flow of your growth in awareness of your true potential.

Remind yourself that for every up, there is a down. For dark, there is light. For a subjective reaction, there is an equal and opposite objective response. Catching your negative thought is step 1. Shifting it to its polar opposite is the second. Practicing is 3rd. And 4th you will note your shifting your mindset has become a habit ... to look for the positive side of the coin automatically.

Keep in mind this quote by Thoreau, "If one advances confidently in the direction of his dreams, and endeavors to live the life which he has imagined, he will meet with a success unexpected in common hours."

Not that we don't need to LEAP out of the gate; that we can take small steps (as long as we keep moving). And that we try, make an effort, or endeavor to live the life we want. Finally, that our success shows up from unexpected sources and at unexpected times.

When you own your purpose, you will reach your potential!

DONNA BROWN

MY AWAKENING CAME while being a consultant for thirty-five years, going from project to project in very, very diverse fields. The projects always left me feeling very embarrassed; I had impostor syndrome before I even knew it was a thing. I would fall into these incredible opportunities with little training or experience, such as fashion designer or garden designer. I worked in television, publishing, all kinds of different things. My dilemma? When people asked me what I did, all I could say is that I don't do much, so I didn't have to say what I was doing at this time. I didn't feel that I had the right to say it because I was not going to do it for long and I was really, really stuck about this.

I think this may be fairly typical of a lot of people. We've been led to believe that there's this one THING – with capital letters – that, once we find it, all of a sudden, everything will click into place for us. We'll have no doubts. Things will be hunky-dory. And we will never question ourselves again. We will go zipping along forever and ever, off into the sunset. I fell for that, hook, line, and sinker – and was conflicted about and struggled with not having that one thing. This went on for a long time – because I kept changing that thing. I had beautiful, exciting and creative jobs with fabulous clients, all of which left me disoriented.

Then I became aware that I had two paths beginning to merge. On the one hand, I had my business issues that were uncomfortable as to my one thing and what I was here to do. At the same time, I had a challenging personal situation and home life that led me to question myself and began to think that there had to be something more than this for me. This was not so great. I grew up thinking of business as one thing, and spiritual and personal development as another and never the twain shall meet. Both sides came crashing down on me, and I had nowhere to turn.

Then my awakening. I had the great, good fortune to recognize and listen to the little voice inside me, saying, "You need to start meditating. You need to start meditating. You need to start meditating." That was very clear, so I started meditating. Then I met a person who does channeling, and found myself asking through rushes of my tears, "What am I here for? What is my purpose?"

The answer came! And it was beautiful and was so freeing that it's something that I share every chance I get. The answer? Life is not a highway. You don't get on at the on-ramp and drive straight till you hit the off ramp. And when said like that, I thought, "Oh, this one thing doesn't sound so great. Who wants to do that?"

Then the invitation was to think of life as a walk in the garden. When you're in a beautiful garden park, you see the flower beds, and certain flowers will attract your attention. Then you enjoy their beauty. You bend down to smell them, look at the bees and the butterflies and the random insects flying around. Then you'll be attracted to something else in the garden. As you meander through this garden, maybe you'll stop at a fountain and listen to the sound of trickling water. If it's a sunny day and you've been walking around for a while, you'll spot some shade under a stand of oak trees and a bench. You walk to the bench and sit down.

Each of these moments is perfect unto itself and doesn't need the moment before it nor the moment after. The moment is there to be explored. Gardens offer themselves to us to enjoy. When I heard this, it felt freeing. I wasn't looking for a magic container or a label for myself that would solve all my embarrassment about what I do. I still struggle with those things. I'm feeling better about it now, and I'm finally comfortable about what I say now about what I do.

On the business side of my life, I now could look past the labels I put on myself. I don't like elevator pitches which I see as labels. It doesn't feel like enough to say I'm a manager or coach, so we created the elevator pitch. It's just more words to remain unsatisfied with the definition of who we've decided who we are.

I think that we all deserve a little more space than an elevator speech and more time. I understand the principle behind the elevator pitch and I kind of tease people about it. But it's really about not confusing who you are with these labels. I've been a fashion designer, I've been a garden designer, I've been a book author, I've been a television presenter or personality – but that doesn't mean that that's all that I am. It's how I choose to see myself at any given moment.

I've come to see these talents as channels for me to relate to the world what I do best. It all comes back to me. That's where the spiritual side of things came into play for me. I am intrinsically a mentor and a visionary. It's effortless and natural for me to tune into a person or to a company and see their piece of the puzzle and where they're supposed to show up in their context, global or local.

My diverse work experience allows me to give my clients particular strategies and tactics to move forward and bring themselves into being more of themselves.

I have found with myself and with my clients, as soon as we see this about ourselves, all of a sudden, our businesses explode. A client, for example, who published a blog that was doing very well, was earning multiple six figures with it, yet was spinning her wheels. She couldn't do more than she was doing and didn't see her way forward. Due to her family needs, it wasn't enough revenue, even while generous.

By helping her understand that what she was really offering was her desire to bring joy to other people. The enjoyment of the small things: chickens, food, organically-made things, handmade, beautiful — like, soaps; it was this enjoyment and this caring for ourselves and caring for others was her real message. When she saw that for herself and realized that she wasn't a blog — but that she was proposing a lifestyle and joy through these things, she launched an e-commerce store. Because of my background in that arena, her monthly income doubled immediately. Then she was on track to eight figures — just like that!

Some may think this sounds crazy and it goes against everything taught in typical business schools. I love this about people. I love when they flourish when they get a new insight. I love people to feel "in the flow," with nothing holding them back. You're not apologizing. You're not toning it down. You're not afraid to explore those bits — even if they're uncomfortable. The people who follow you, who buy your products, who listen to you, who work with you, are attracted to exactly that. It's not a new concept yet it is a profound one, and it's a significant shift from the way business was taught years ago.

When I finally stepped back from all these labels and containers and looked underneath, I asked myself what was I doing for my clients? What was I doing ... whether for a food service company or the LaScala Operate Theater or a big fashion brand. I realized that my real gift was understanding what a company or a business can become holistic with their unique place in the world, and how they are showing up.

When you understand this about yourself, that you are not what you do, you can even shift your direction on a dime. It could be business coaching, life coaching, working for a non-profit or provide physical products. I advise people to look carefully at what they've done in the past and include the best of what they used to do in what they are doing now, if possible. Change what you say from "I don't do that anymore because I'm doing this. Oh, I don't do that anymore. Now I do this." It's not necessary to turn your back on your own experiences. There was something when you took that job or took that client that led you to think it was a good idea. And it was at that time.

There are a lot of entrepreneurs that are doing several things that they love, and for them, it's very scattered. They don't understand yet how to bring it all together. I can see people physically relax when I say, "Well, can you see that underneath this maybe there is the common thread of how you show you up and how you serve the world." This allows them to be a little bit freer with their actual so-called business model, offers, products, and services.

Trust yourself. Trust your voice. Give yourself a little bit of space and time to figure out what it all means. You may not change your actual business. You may stay as a web designer or a business coach. I believe though that you'll find that your language will change: how you speak to your ideal client changes. When I discover something new about myself, and it makes me happy and more fulfilled, all of a sudden my language becomes deeper. I connect with clients on a much deeper level, where the real connection and the actual selling without selling takes place. You're not selling the service – you're sell-ing what's underneath it, which is what they need.

I've heard people say they want five more clients or to earn six fig-ures, but that's not really what they want. They want to feel fulfilled, and joyful and living a life of purpose. Our big goals have us think we don't know how to get there. You only need a short process to get you into action with the smallest thing that you could do to move toward your goal.

Do enough of those small things and when you look back, all of a sudden, you'll see that your business will be gaining momentum.

My gift below is about how to achieve any goal you want. I have learned we may tend to edit our own goals before we even allow our-selves to want them, hence, my gift.

Download Donna's Gift HERE:
http://donnabrown.com/goals/

DONNA BROWN BIOGRAPHY

Donna Brown is a super-scaling growth strategist, business mentor, intuitive visionary and international speaker with over thirty years experience as a consultant in such diverse fields as fashion, interior and garden design, lifestyle, events, food service, publishing, tv, editorial projects, coaching and mentoring.

With each client, whether entrepreneur, corporation or foundation, she provides long-term and profound visions of what they can become to truly fulfill their mission and purpose in the world, and with them creates the strategies and tactics to execute this vision.

Her spiritual journey in Buddhist studies and her experience with corporate-based mindfulness have led her to understand her biggest successes in business stem from the combination of her spiritual practices, experience and strategy.

It is this unique combination of business and awareness that represents the trend and shift for businesses of the future, big or small. Shifting the paradigms around business itself, to perceive it as a form and extension of our human flourishing combined with her visionary strategies are the secret weapons she uses to unleash powerful entrepreneurs, corporations and foundations to help them create unique and profitable businesses with global impact.

AIMEE CHANDLER

MY AWAKENING MOMENT is not only the source of my own personal development, but it's also actually the source of my professional development, too. It lead me to what I am doing today; helping busy women find ways to be healthy without having to make huge, significant changes in their lifestyle.

A couple of years ago while in my mid-40s, I was a wife and a mother of two young kids. I was working full-time in a high-level sales career, was teaching fitness classes and had personal training clients. It also felt sometimes like I was volunteering for 50 million different things in my community, and my children's too!

I had that busy syndrome going on. I was hyper-focused on eating well and exercising regularly because that's what I am trained in. I had been doing this for many years and becoming a mom made me want to set an even better example for my kids. But in reality, I was super stressed, attempting to find a balance between family and work time – and even some 'me' time. I knew giving back to myself was important, yet was just so hard to fit into my schedule. Then I got to a point where I felt like there just had to be a better way of living.

I also had this back-of-the-mind nagging feeling that for the amount of effort I was putting into eating healthy and exercising, over-exercising, working out so many hours during the week, I really should be getting better results. I admit, I wasn't overweight or suffering from a major health issue. I know a lot of women are going through this, whether chronic fatigue or fibromyalgia or busy syndrome stress. While nothing significant, you might agree that you know when you're not in that right place physically or mentally, and you know it could be better. That was me.

I was spending so much time and energy exercising harder and longer — and thinking that what had worked in my 20s and 30s would work the same way. I believed that this would get me there, even if I had to do more of it. But unfortunately, it wasn't working. I also was in a bit of denial. I think a lot of women can relate to this: I was using my commitment to exercise as kind of my excuse for being able to still indulge in treats and having that glass of wine several nights a week. Life was so busy and stressful, after all! I would rationalize that, "oh, you know what? I earned this. I deserve this because I powered through and I worked so hard to get through this crazy week. I can treat myself. I can do this." Which, you can, to some degree — and then there's that line you cross to consider, which causes you to become counterproductive.

If you follow StrengthsFinder [https://www.amazon.com/dp/B001CDZZI6/] or other personality profile tests available, I am an Activator by nature; I get to the point! And so I did! Finally, I got sick of just thinking about it and overanalyzing it and going over it and over. And I remember thinking to myself, "You've just got to do something about this!" Right.

I took action and dove back into my Master's program training. I got involved in the wellness organizations that I belong to, to try and figure out how I could reach my full potential and finally maximize my results, for all the effort I was investing into my healthy lifestyle and healthy living.

My college roommate life coach. We went away for a weekend together to an industry convention. And it was spending time with her for a whole weekend that had me decide to get into action. Having somebody else appreciate me for who I was who enjoyed me so much, made me wonder why am I so hard on myself. She was my reflection.

I realized that if I could change my mindset, the world would be my oyster. Going on that, I started doing my research. As I got deeper into understanding the physiological changes that happened to women after 40, going into peri-menopause, then menopause. I had gone into menopause at a young age, so I knew about them. I also discovered the importance of mindset in terms of stress reduction, changing your behavior, and being able to reach your goals.

That is truly where my awakening began – with my girlfriend, my life coach brought it to my attention. Once I was researching things seemed to blossom. I started reading Mindset by Carol Dweck and as I read, flashes would go off. It was helping me turn my mindset around.

So once you had this awakening, if you will – and I love it that you were with someone else.

One of the challenges is that there is so much information out there – whether it's in a magazine, on a TV show, on the news, online, about how to eat healthily and how to exercise. What I have found through my coaching and from my own experience is, yes, you do have to find what works for you. And there are many options that you can try – yet ultimately, you only continue to be successful if you have the right mindset for consistency and moderation. That doesn't come from an exercise program or nutrition. That's in your mind and setting yourself up in a positive place. That's treating yourself well and being kind to yourself.

I have a model I share with my clients: There's no such thing as a good or a bad choice. It's a good, better, or a best choice. Because when we take away that negative word, bad, it just opens up possibilities, allowing us to explore what works well for us, without having to feel like we were successful or we failed. Because there's no such thing as failure. Failure is just that opportunity to learn and grow.

I felt like I was born with an all-or-nothing attitude about achievement and reaching success in life. It's probably more learned behavior than something you're born with.

It served me well for most of my life, allowing me to reach many successes and achieve things that I was looking for. But as I started to mature and raise children and notice certain behaviors from those successes, I realized that this all-or-nothing attitude was holding me back — especially when it came to my wellness. Since twenty-five, I always used exercise as my way of handling my weight management.

I was not consistent, however. I did not live in moderation. I would say to myself "oh, I could never diet like my girlfriend." I'd go away for the weekend, and my girlfriends would all be talking about the South Beach or Atkins Diet. I would automatically, in my head, be saying to myself, "Nope, nope, nope, I will never be able to do that. I don't have the kind of willpower they have. And, if I can't be great at it, I'm not doing it at all!" And it was that all-or-nothing attitude that was not allowing me to explore.

So after some twenty years of this attitude, I finally realized it just wasn't serving me. I needed to start to think about progress over perfection. That's really what I help my clients to understand from that mindset perspective. It's not about being perfect all the time. It's about watching yourself start at point A and move at your unique pace; not that of anyone else.

My first step — when I had that awakening and realized that this all-or-nothing attitude was holding me back, was to embrace a trial-and-error approach to life and in my wellness and healthy lifestyle living. I admit that my fear of being perfect is still strong. It's still a work in progress for me.

Once I started making changes in my eating and exercise practices, I finally gained the confidence in myself that I could awaken that infinite potential in myself. It's about how you I felt inside about myself. It's not about others. It's finding that inner light that makes you say, "You know what? I can do this. There's more to life." Or, "Why am I holding back from allowing myself to experience something new and different?"

I met a naturopath, and I began to follow him online. One day I received his newsletter featuring an article he wrote about life being a series of trial-and-error events! What hit home about the article was all the examples he referred to where we use trial and error. Choosing our college major, career, to have children, how to raise them. There's no manual or instruction book to life. It's all trial-and-error! You try something and see if it works. If yes, there's a benefit. If you don't, you decide to change and move on.

Figuring out the nutrition and exercise routine that fit my lifestyle and my body type was the key. That's what I help other women figure out. What works for your neighbor or your sister or your friend down the street might not work for you. And you've got to be able to have the mindset strategies – and basic scientific information to move forward and use that trial-and-error method to figure out what does work for you and your lifestyle.

When I embraced this change – I was quiet about it. I thought, "You know, I'm not going to announce to the world that I'm doing anything. I'm just going to make some changes subtly." The truth is, I still was in a little bit of fear of failure. I didn't want to put it out there that I was doing something different – and not be successful. I had to get over that. I wanted to make small tweaks because I didn't want to overwhelm myself with a total overhaul.

So in terms of my eating, I made some simple changes –cutting out processed foods, adding more protein, healthy fats, veggie-based carbs – to fill me up from meal to meal. And it was the kind of food that I needed to fuel my exercise.

No food was off-limits. Certain foods naturally became lower on the priority scale. I intentionally made more of an effort to fill up on the good stuff first – to then determine whether or not, "Okay, every once in a while, I'll have that cookie or that glass of wine," as opposed to having that be the first thing I thought about.

For my exercise, I learned that scientifically that my hardcore approach to exercise was increasing my cortisol levels. And cortisol is our stress hormone that is responsible for holding on to body fat – especially around the midsection. Many women exercise diligently and have small arms and legs, yet over time, they continue to build fat around that middle section of their body and remain confused as to why they aren't losing weight there.

They eat well, they exercise all the time, and yet they're so frustrated they don't even know what to do. They're exhausted, they're hungry all the time – and they can't lose that weight.

That was the key for me: As soon as I realized I was over exercising and I cut back and walked more, purely leisure walking, no power walking, just appreciating nature, to de-stress – literally, the body fat just burnt right off. I couldn't believe it. And the bonus? I had more time in my day to spend with my family, to be working in the business that I was starting. I was spending less time exercising, more time doing things that I wanted to do. My stress levels came down.

When I made those changes, and I started to get results, as I mentioned, I had not told anybody what I was doing. Then, it seemed like all of a sudden, my clients, my family, my friends were like, "Wait a second, what's going on here? You got to give me your secret." Because we women, we all want to share those secrets, right?

Next, I realized that my talking about what I was doing (at my level), was going over people's heads. So many women think that there has to be this dramatic change in their life. When I simplified it, I created a guide to follow. Many women are still stuck in the old mentality of "I've got to work out harder and longer." "And I'm going to punish myself when I do cheat."

Then they wake up the next day after indulging in pizza and wine, or going out for burgers with their family and wake up in a panic because they believe they did something bad the night before when in reality, that's making it worse – and making their body want to hold onto that. So this guide contains the four simple strategies I used. This is how I guide all my clients concerning the balance between nutrition, exercise, and mindset. It's LEAN because we're trying to get lean! LEAN stands for Lift weights; Eat more protein; Alleviate stress; and set non-negotiables. I no longer believe in deprivation diets and that all food groups can be a part of your daily life. That's why I have non-negotiables. This is how my approach differs from other health coaches.

There are many effective programs available, and because they're so restrictive in terms of no sugar, the no caffeine, no carbs, and no fat, not everybody can do it. Same thing with exercise; specific, strict, exercise. We can do this for 21 days or 30 days and get those results. But then, what happens after that?

We go into it with a mindset that this is temporary. "Oh, I'm just going to do this for 30 days. I can do anything for 30 days, no matter how restrictive it is." And then, we get to the end of those 30 days and what happens? We go right back to our old ways.

My gift below is designed to help you stop over exercising.

Download Aimee's Gift HERE:
https://aimeechandlerwellness.lpages.co/ultimate-guide-to-stop-over-exercising/

AIMEE CHANDLER BIOGRAPHY

Aimee Chandler has been a wellness professional for over 25 years, helping hundreds of women create healthier lifestyles through exercise, fundamental nutrition, stress management and self appreciation.

She has a master's degree in Exercise Science, holds numerous certifications in exercise and coaching but more importantly she has a life story, which is probably pretty similar to yours.

At 47, she was a mom of 2 young kids, working a fulltime job, starting her own business and already in menopause! Fighting the effects of hormonal changes on a daily basis by exercising and restricting calories to maintain her ideal body wasn't working anymore and she knew it was time to make a lifestyle change.

By letting go of her "all or nothing" attitude and focusing on progress over perfection, she was finally able to reach her goals and actually enjoy the journey of healthy living instead of feeling like it was a chore.

She has taken her knowledge and experience to the online world to help even more women find health, happiness and a body they love, no matter how busy they are.

As a self diagnosed "busy syndrome" sufferer she believes that slowing down and being kind to yourself has an emotional and physical benefit that is the key to overall wellness.

JEANETTE CHASWORTH

FOR ME, MY awakening was all about color. Before I tell you about it, take a moment and imagine yourself as butterfly — strong, beautiful, feminine, wings spread out, flying through the sky, free, independent. What color are your wings? Red, blue, purple? Do you have spots? Do you have stripes? Each one is unique, beautiful.

No matter your choice, each color has its power, its strength. I refer to myself as the "Color Whisperer." I love working with people who are ready to re-create their lives by re-creating their home environment. There are colors all around us which we take for granted ... "Oh, it's just this color. It looks pretty on me. I feel pretty in it." I have learned that it's so much deeper than that.

Today, I feel confident, awakened, and wonderful in being who I am. It wasn't always that way. For a long time I felt small, depressed, and uncomfortable in my skin. I didn't like what I saw in the mirror. It didn't matter what was there; I didn't like it. I look back now at pictures of me at that time, and I was pretty. I didn't like my reflection regardless. When I was a year old, my father died. I was, of course, unable to comprehend what was going on. The brain cells just weren't developed yet. All I knew is that this man who was so vital to me suddenly was gone. So I retreated into myself.

I wouldn't let anybody near me – especially men. No man was going to come near me. No man was going to hurt me again. The grief, when it happens – when it occurs deeply, is like somebody reaches into your chest, rips out your heart and leaves you standing there, wondering, "How do I keep going? How do I take the next step? Why is the world continuing to turn?" I looked at other people in similar situations and thought "How can they keep taking that next step? I don't know how."

Retreating into myself, I hid from family and friends, and the world. Because I had to – I had to build a cocoon around myself. I had to protect myself. I had to fill that hole my father left again and re-create myself.

If this is you, ask yourself this question, "Who are you for the next part of this life? Who are you without that experience, without that person in your life?" I found the way to move forward is to take the good things; the love, the good experiences – the strength that you learned from it – and fill yourself with love, thereby filling that space. While love never dies, you still have to re-create you. Maybe for you, it's a new haircut or a new outfit. But when it's deep, you might have to change your surroundings or your home environment.

So there I was, at a year old, inside the cocoon I built for myself. I knew how to do that. I didn't know, however, how to do the rest. Because my brain cells hadn't yet developed, I grew up in a cocoon of grief. I'd fight against the sadness which said to me, "Play small, don't be yourself. Don't stretch," than me saying to grief, "You're not going to get the best of me. I'm going to take charge. I'm going to do this anyway. I'm here to be me." And I stepped up and fought it, and I stretched against that cocoon. While I couldn't break it, it did get thinner. I could see other people living without a cocoon. I saw what it looked like – but I didn't know how to create it for me.

And then, something amazing happened. My awakening! I discovered color!

I was going to school for Interior Design, and we had a class on the Psychology of Color. That class was the catalyst that changed how I looked at the world forever. I learned that color affects how we think, what we feel, what we do – and every aspect of our lives.

Let me give you a few examples. When you go to the airport, you see a lot of blue. The reason? Blue helps you trust, and with a lot of people afraid to travel by air, they can be nervous. So blue is a great color to use. It also helps you forget the passage of time. When you have long layovers and arrive early, the color blue is a great thing to make your trip to the airport less stressful.

Blue shows up in hospitals, especially in hospital gowns. The reason? Blue also has the innate ability to help retard disease – so why not use it when you're sick? Another example which everybody loves, because it's easy to understand, is the use of color in restaurants. Diners like Denny's and fast food places, like McDonald's and Burger King, use what dominant colors for decorating?

If you said reds, yellows, and oranges, you answered correctly. These colors have high vibrations, which make you hungry and eat more. It's advisable to leave as soon as you finish your meal.

In contrast, coffeehouses like Starbucks and Peets use different colors for an entirely opposite effect. They want you to linger. They want to be your go-to place, and they want you to stay longer – because they know you'll buy more. So you're going to see more blues, more greens, and golds. You might see a little 'pumpkin,' or if you see a red, it's a muted red. We are all going to be affected by colors that make you want to stay.

The next time you go out to eat, you'll be aware of what "What they want you to do!"

When I was in my 20s, I had asthma, and I engaged a metaphysical healer. I didn't know what metaphysics was at that time. All I knew is that he said he could fix my asthma. He shared with me that all those tears that I had as a baby that never got cried out when my father died, so got stuck in my lungs. That's why I couldn't breathe. He was able to release those tears. Two days later, all of a sudden I started to sob uncontrollably – tears began flowing like rain. I went to the bathroom to get a towel because this was not a tissue kind of cry! I grabbed the blue and pink towel – both calming colors – and my head said, "No, green. I want green." "Okay," so I grabbed the green towel. Why do you think green was so important that day? Green is a color that helps you deal with change.

Green is also a color that is emotionally healing – what an incredible thing to help me get through this. I sobbed for three hours that day. My cocoon finally broke, yet I still didn't have my beautiful wings. I got part of that hole filled, yet I still didn't know how to earn my wings and fly.

What I learned from this experience was that there was a much deeper level of understanding color that I just had to find more about; it was much more than what my teachers had taught me.

Next, I discovered The Personality of Color. That's where I got my wings. I learned that we're each beautiful pieces of art with an energy unique to us and intrinsically our own. When I found my unique 'color blueprint,' what my energy was, and my core beauty was – I began to look in the mirror and smile. I found my wings. I emerged as a Monarch butterfly with dark orange color and markings that I love.

Here's how this works. Pink is my creative color. Today, I'm in my creative passion mode. I may want to be calm, so I select pink. This is my go-on-a-date color: soft, subtle, romantic. When I want to be more powerful, I wear green. Every day, I can use color to enhance whatever it is I'm going to do – and make me, more me, making you see more of who I am.

Gray is a trendy color right now. It seems like everybody loves gray. I need texture. I need color. When I have gold in a garment with a pretty fabric, it does nothing for my skin. So trendy doesn't always mean it's for you. Here's another example. Blue jeans go with everything, right? Not for me. And white. White's everybody friend. White goes with everything, right? White does not go with me at all. I can feel the energy draining out of my body, just having something white in front of me. So having the right colors around you can make a huge difference. It can go a long way to build you up, or it can also bring you down.

Your home is a reflection of you. Ever said, "My house is such a mess, I can't think?" It's true. You can't think clearly when your surroundings are a mess. Cleaning your house will help you think better. When you're grieving, it's the same way: Your house needs to reflect who you are. You have worked hard for your home. It can and will be as challenging for working on you.

Meet Marie.

Recently separated, and while her husband had moved out, there was still a lot of the energy present that didn't work between them in their home, and she didn't know how to fix it. Whether it's a separation, a divorce, or death, the master bedroom is the most intimate of spaces. With such a massive change in her life, Marie had to re-create herself as an individual. She was no longer part of a couple.

As I entered her bedroom, it was a beautiful, healing, sage green, which wasn't working for her. She didn't need green that at that point. She was a Monarch butterfly like me. She needed gold. She needed joy in her life which had been missing for so long. And she needed a strong color to support her, to hold her, to give her the strength to step into her new self.

We changed the drapes, the bedding, and a few things throughout the house. But the master bedroom was key – and the energy of the right colors seemed to start bouncing around the bedroom. And it bubbled up inside Marie! She was becoming more alive. She broke her cocoon of grief – and she became herself, her true self.

I was in the interior design field when I saw how this personality of color affected the deeper part of me. I declared then and there, "This is my passion because I believe that colors heal."

One of the first steps I took was to learn about my own colors, and when I saw how powerful they were and how great I looked and felt in my clothes, I decided I'd take those concepts and use them in people's homes to help them.

I learned the metaphysical healing potential, and for me, design is a form of healing. It's not just about making a house pretty. It's about creating an energetic environment that gives you the strength to do more.

That's the magical thing about this technique that I use with my clients. You don't have to know your blueprint. You don't have to know what you want to be for the next part of your life. I build the reflection of it, of your beauty, of your essence — for you, and then you step into it. That's exactly what I did for myself: I stepped into my calling ... to help others, to heal others — and help them get through tough times.

A mom brought her little daughter to me who had dyslexia. In her bedroom, she had big pink and white stripes on her wall. She was having nightmares about 9/11 all the time. The big stripes were waving; her dyslexia disallowed her to see straight lines. So she wouldn't sleep in her bed! How many doctors would've looked at her bedroom as I did? How many pills was this girl eventually going to have to be taking to manage her dyslexia? One can of paint changed all that.

Orange is an excellent color for creativity. Here's what I would like to propose: is, you need to start somewhere, so listen to your gut, not your head. I don't care what the books say. I don't care what anybody else says.

Have you ever gone through a situation where suddenly you're wearing a different color? Just, all of a sudden, you're attracted to the blue or green?

Your body needed that. Your body knew what it needed.

So listen to what your gut says about color. It's hard for most people to do — but if you listen, you can't go wrong.

My gift below is an ebook, Breaking Your Cocoon with Color. That's why I'm called the Color Whisperer. The impact can be huge with buying a $20 single can of paint when it's the right color for you!

Download Jeanette's Gift HERE:
https://www.thecolorwhisperer.com/breaking-your-cocoon

JEANETTE CHASWORTH BIOGRAPHY

Jeanette Chatsworth's clients have nicknamed her "The Color Whisperer" because of her intuitive approach to creating unique homes for her clients. When starting a new project, she first listens to the needs and desires of both the client and the house. Instead of fitting her style into a project, she utilizes her intuition and design knowledge to create an environment that weaves together each client's unique tastes, preferences and functional needs to create a space that reflect the client's personality.

After working with Jeanette, clients describe their rooms as "visual expressions of their personality." Their homes move from feeling chaotic to feeling more like a sanctuary. There is a sense of peace and comfort created by colors and textures that now harmonize with the energy of the client—and with their home.

A frequent guest speaker for various radio talk shows, Jeanette loves sharing her passion with all those who want to better understand what color communicates in our everyday lives. Aside from being elected President of the Pasadena Chapter of the American Society of Interior Designers (ASID) from 2011-2012, Jeanette's work has been featured in several industry publications such as Fabulous Floors Magazine, Arroyo Monthly, La Canada Home, Arts & Crafts Home, and several Best of Houzz awards. Her first book is What's Color Got to Do with It?

MEGAN DAVIES

I HAD STARTED and was running several businesses myself, yet I wasn't feeling fulfilled. My awakening moment boiled down to three separate, pivotal moments that happened to me.

First was the loss of my best friend, Kyle. He was absolutely amazing. Best friends since grade 3, Kyle was always that person that I could talk to about everything and anything. He was that kind of friend that would build me up, light me up inside – and I never felt afraid of being myself around him. Losing him was devastating to me.

Next, a couple of years later, I lost my grandma. And my grandma – like Kyle – was the one I could go to and talk to. She was always there for me.

And then, a couple of months after I lost my grandma – just this past December – my dad was diagnosed with lung cancer.

After that, I had a massive breakdown. It made me stop short, take a deep breath, and ask these questions: "Where was I in my life? What was I doing? Was I feeling fulfilled? Was I showing up for others the way that these three people in my life had shown up for me? Was I touching other people around me the way that those people had touched my life?" And I had to be honest with myself: unfortunately,

I was not. I wasn't feeling fulfilled in the businesses that I was running – even though I loved being in business. I just felt like my heart was not connecting with the people that I wanted to connect with. I wasn't using my heart and my energy to build up people around me – which is really what I wanted to do.

Knowing that I wasn't fulfilled in my heart, that I wasn't touching people, and wanting to work with them, I took my first step. I found a coach who was doing what I wanted to do. Someone who was out there in a big way and had the skills I wanted to develop to work specifically with women and moms.

From there, I reviewed the content that I had been creating for years, thinking like a coach, before my dad's diagnosis. I was looking for a way to use this content to help connect me with the women I felt called to work with.

While creating my three businesses, I had documented all the things that helped me over the years. All the steps (and missteps) that I had taken to make them successful. And with each new business I created, it became easier and easier, because I knew the formula. I knew the secret sauce or the magic recipe. I knew how to make it happen by connecting the dots.

Now I am doing what I dreamed of doing ... connecting with other entrepreneurs – women and moms – and helping them put those plans into action, and really, take their passions; what they love doing, what they feel fulfilled in doing – and helping create and turn that passion into a business, so that they can have a life that lights them up – that makes them feel fulfilled. Just like I feel when helping them.

Business One is a concrete finishing company.

Business Two started because we had been renting vans to get rid of concrete on job sites and we stumbled onto some good deal on a truck and bins. Investing in them created a whole new business.

Business Three: Wholesale motorcycle inner tubes in Colombia, South America. Lots of motorcycles there.

Now for the 'secret sauce.' It's made up of specific steps that, once you know them, makes it super easy to start, create – and then re-create from there. I believe the secret is knowing those steps – knowing how to put it all together, and then knowing how and when to take action and apply them, that is the magic.

So I first hired a coach, then began to look at my existing written content in starting a business to help others start theirs. I learned the process doesn't need to be complicated. I know that getting into business can feel incredibly overwhelming, particularly when you're not sure exactly where to start. Because I had never coached anyone before, I decided that my first step needed to be to hire a coach, so I could learn the steps I needed to take in my new business.

I realized that we don't know how many tomorrows there are and I didn't want to wait anymore. I needed to take action now because I wanted to show up. I wanted to feel fulfilled. I wanted to lead my life the way that I felt in my heart I was meant to live my life. And that's feeling fulfilled, helping other people – and showing up fully.

My best advice if your story is like mine is to recognize your awakening and take action, get in the right mindset – and believe in yourself. Once you have that belief in yourself, it helps build momentum for everything. There is plenty to go around in the universe – and once you have that belief within yourself to go after it, the universe magically delivers what you manifest and what you believe.

I have found that the 3 C's, Clarity, Courage, and Commitment, are what it takes to be successful. You'll find them in my Gift below.

Download Megan's Gift HERE:
http://megan-speaks.com/awakenyourinfinitepotential

MEGAN DAVIES BIOGRAPHY

Megan Davies is a heart-centered serial entrepreneur who has created and grown multiple, multi-six figure businesses. She has worked with brands you know like Disney, Paramount, NASA, Coca-Cola, Shell and many more. She has spoken for audiences throughout Canada and the United States sharing more than 15 years of experience-based knowledge in Sales, Marketing & Business with some of the nation's greatest thinkers from fortune 500 Companies, Start-ups and every-one in between.

Megan believes that with drive, determination and great ideas, entrepreneurs can and will change the world one great idea at a time. She has made it her mission to help entrepreneurs create that change by providing up-to-date education and tools to make your life easier, your business run more efficiently, and most importantly, won't let you give up! She loves to help motivate entrepreneurs, like you, to create and live a life you love so you can ultimately live free.

Megan loves spending time with her family, including two beautiful daughters that light up her life motivating her to do better and be better every day. She also loves fine wine, writing in the third person, and inspiring entrepreneurs to be the change they want to see.

ESHA HERBERT-DAVIS

MY AWAKENING HAPPENED in 2015. For years prior, I was exhausted and stuck in the corporate rat race. That's when I started taking Trinidad Carnival trips, a local festival on the islands of Trinidad and Tobago in the Caribbean. My first trips were with my girlfriends. We went every year to experience this amazing festival, have a blast – and then come back to our regular life. So it started before 2015. Organizing these adventure trips for myself and my girlfriends soon parlayed into a business. Then I began organizing trips for other people – and of course, had a great time ...living my daydream and having fun with it.

It was in 2015 when we sent out our annual survey at the end of every Trinidad Carnival trip to ask people, "How was it? Did you have a great time? Is there anything we can do differently? Is there anything that we can to do more to make this event more amazing for you?" We got a lot of fantastic feedback from Raven, one of our clients. What she told us completely blew us away. Here's an excerpt of what she has sent.

"I must say, thank you to Esha and Tariq" (Tariq is my husband and business partner), "for all of your hard work and dedication in putting together this 2015 Carnival trip. It was amazing. I must shout out the rest of the UTC crew for holding down this group of vagabonds and making sure everything was taken care of every step of the way. Love, love, love to each of you. Thank you for looking out for each other and many times, for me. Your love, sincere concern, and endless joy is deeply appreciated – and inspires me to be a better person. You are beautiful."

Now, here's the part that blew me away. "Finally, I must say thank you from the bottom of my heart to Esha and Grace (another member on your team) for putting my concerns to rest about how I felt I wasn't slim enough to be in a costume. Sadly, I spent decades hating my body and trying to hide it all by packing on the pounds. Funny thing is, no matter how big I get, my shape remains. Ha ha ha. Anywho, I've been working hard on body image and self-love for the last year – and the self-love and confidence I saw within the UTC crew, all the sincere compliments I received from the crew and others – and witnessing a bazillion people in all shapes, sizes, colors, etc. just really enjoy themselves with no judgments and no apologies, for being who they are – really helped me break through. I'm not sure if Carnival was meant to be a breakthrough, spiritual or a healing type of event – but it was for me. And I am forever grateful. Thank you."

My Awakening was that this was not just an average trip. It touched my heart because it certainly was not intended that way. Raven and other clients since then, year after year, were experiencing their, by accepting their body image and being proud of their bodies – and being confident in their own skin. That's what touched me; knowing that that was the experience that I was giving them. This wasn't a trip. It was an experience.

My first step was to rebrand! While we started doing Ultimate Trinidad Carnival in 2012, by 2015 –we were one of the pioneers of this type of experience. By 2015, there were a few other similar businesses that popped up, trying to do the same thing. I knew then it was time for us to rebrand and differentiate what we were bringing to the table and determining our value.

Step 1. I began reviewing websites and information from other premium trips available because we were offering a premium experience. This was a turnkey adventure; all of the research done, all of the booking done, all about taking care of you. Getting to Trinidad, traveling with you, making sure that you were safe in that environment. So it dictated billing ourselves as a premium company.

Step 2. With the rebranding came a more premium look and feel. We needed a logo. The website needed to look as premium as what we were offering. The language had to change. All of that was necessary to build out the business. Who would we attract? Because if it was a premium experience, we needed to demand a premium price. So we wanted someone who would not mind paying a premium price for a premium experience.

It's important to note that I didn't do it all by myself. Step 3 was building a team. We had a graphic designer, website consultants, and all of that things went along with creating that premium brand and that premium web presence.

These adventures are a thoroughly unique experience. Everyone is there to have fun. As you know, the high vibration and the joy and the fun-having and the laughter and everything and the partying –it's a fever pitch. Everyone is just there to have a great time. Parties to attend, all-inclusive, all-you-can-eat, and all-you-can-drink. Where else do you go, and you can go to the bar and drink whatever you what and eat whatever you? It's all topped off with a Carnival parade – where you can put on a beautiful, albeit skimpy costumes with lots of feathers, lots of bling. You have your Carnival makeup done – and you look gorgeous and stunning. Now you are ready to party in the street! And then you go home.

I have learned that as women, we do not give ourselves permission to invest in ourselves – whether a trip or working with a coach to help build our businesses.

I'm a big proponent of "just do it" (Nike) before your brain gets in there and the self-talk starts, "Well, you can't afford this. You can't do this. You can't do that." You don't give yourself permission to do it – you just Decide, then do it. Decide, then DO IT. That's all you need to do.

A point about your daydreams and how they come into play with your awakening.

First, take stock of your daydreams. Write them down. "Do you daydream?" There's so many of us who do not. "In that daydream, what would you do to have fun?" This is important to me when I reflect on my life – and I look back at what I accomplished; the high points of my life. I was always having fun while achieving those things, those great things like starting my business, meeting my husband, having my son, and moving to North Carolina. These were all things that happened while I was having fun. The impact is so significant on your life when you are having fun with what you're doing. So daydream.

Carnival is my joy. Trinidad Carnival is my joy. That's what makes me happy. Whatever your daydream is that makes you happy and brings you that joy, you are guaranteed to have an awakening while jotting down these daydreams, for sure.

Download Esha's Gift HERE:
https://mailchi.mp/eventsbyashe.com/3-ways-to-stop-feeling-exhausted-worksheet

ESHA HERBERT-DAVIS BIOGRAPHY

Esha Herbert-Davis is the co-owner of Events by Ashé, LLC, a company that specializes in unique and life-changing Caribbean experiences.

The most popular experience offered is the annually sold out Ultimate Trinidad Carnival where professional women immerse themselves in the local Carnival culture with 5 days of partying, parading in a beautiful costume, getting dirty with paint and mud at J'ouvert (pronounced jou-vay) and relaxing at the beach!

Esha is the author of the soon to be released "Confessions of a Carnivalista," is a speaker and also mentors other women to help them find their joy.

LESLIE FLOWERS

I THOUGHT A long time about which awakening of mine would mean the most to you, the reader, to spur you into action to step into your inherent and infinite potential.

It was late in 2007, while I was still working in corporate and the movie The Secret came out. It was an unexpected, runaway success. No one expected it to be as significant and have the impact that it did worldwide. Right then I started a Meetup group called The Secret Society. The purpose of our monthly meeting was to take a look at all the people featured in the movie; all the practices and practitioners.

Still working in corporate America, I had that salary I could count on. And I'm loving running these meetings, leading the discussions, and having Law of Attraction events. The Law of Attraction was one hot topic, you may remember. I kept asking myself, "I wonder if there's a way to make money doing this?" That would be awesome.

I learned then to always be on the lookout for the answers to my questions and that the answers are often unexpected. One day while checking my email – a messages came in from a stranger. Now, think about this: In 2007, if an email came in, you didn't open it if you didn't know the person. Something told me to open it. So going against what

I knew about our environment, I opened it anyway. There was a short message with a link. Oh, my goodness, 2007 – never, never, never click on a link from an email from someone. This was the number-one rule. And still is!

Well you guessed it. I clicked the link. It landed me on a very simple website, belonging to Bob Proctor. What I didn't know then is that Proctor is still a world-class expert in *Think and Grow Rich* by Napoleon Hill.

All I knew about Proctor was I had just seen him for the first time as the grandfatherly narrator in the movie *The Secret*. I had no idea where I was going by clicking that link, but it became interesting what happened next.

At that moment, my first step was to pick up the phone and call the number on the web page. It was instinctive that I clicked the link when I knew I shouldn't. That was my first awakening – you ask for something. It arrives in an unexpected way, and there was something within me that, even all those years ago, that said, "Go ahead. Do it anyway. Find out what this is. This could be your answer." And so it was.

The hitch was, and of course there would be one, was that I could buy a business-in-the-box and show up the following Spring for a training with Bob Proctor in Florida. I did show up in March 2008.

The Hitch: They told me on that first call that I needed $16,000!! And I had $500. And before I hung up, I said, "I'll see you in March." Now, I had no clue how I was going to get that money. And by the way, they also said to me, "You're going to do a Mastermind on Think and Grow Rich before you arrive in March." My question was, "What's a Mastermind? And what the heck is Think and Grow Rich?" So I knew nothing about it. Nothing! But I was moved in that direction, without knowing why.

I had $500 and needed $16,000 to do what I wanted. Whenever you really, really, really know something is right – and you focus on that, I've learned this from my clients, you will get it. You simply don't always know by when.

You only have to look at a toddler going after something. That was me with buying into this business! The toddler will risk life and limb to get that cookie right before dinner – even if there are threats, etc., and scolding. So it was that hell-bent toddler part of me that said, "I knew this was it." I knew I was supposed to be in this business. And sure enough, by March, through a windfall, the money showed up, and I was in West Palm Beach with hundreds of other dreamers like me.

That was my first awakening. It went against everything that I knew intellectually – yet, awakenings, I've learned over the last 10 years and from all the people I've interviewed and my own clients – that it really takes something to override those beliefs that we can't do something and understanding that this is really what we need and want to be doing.

"I shouldn't click the link. I shouldn't open the email." My intuition overrode that, and I allowed it. That's one of the indications you are getting a nudge or hint or message from the Universe – when you feel a pushback that this isn't the right thing to do – yet, you're sensing that it is. One thought or voice is the voice of your beliefs; what you have learned to believe in through repetition and operate out of all your life, bumping up against the feeling that the universe is sending you a message. And in this case, I'm grateful that I took those steps because the other thought or voice is that of the Universe. There are two voices; your own and that of the universe or creator.

Spring 2008, I was at the training with hundreds of other dreamers and invested $5,000 more (that I paid monthly) to work every week with exemplary mentors in a variety of fields. Unfortunately, only two or three out of every 100 of the folks in training that spring ever followed through with growing a business. I know why now ... but did not know why then ... the 3% had a deep desire to override the routine obstacles in starting a business. They were hyper-focused and determined to do whatever it took to grow a business. Above all, they were willing to do what it takes. I was willing.

I have learned from my clients that everyone wants things and they are even willing to invest financially, yet only a few are willing to do what it takes. Having to come up with $16,000 when I had $500 was an obstacle. Yet my drive and desire were so great; I was so sure this was my next step – that I just left it up to the universe and just like that two-year-old, ended up with the cookie and probably got dessert, too, that night.

You may think these awakenings can't happen to you and that only certain people get them and recognize them. I've learned that is not true. Everyone has these nudges and awakening moments. The key is learning to identify them. They are present when you hear yourself say, "Oh, what a coincidence," or "You know, I just thought I wanted that," or "I've thought about that for a long, and it finally showed up." No, it's NOT A COINCIDENCE. It's synchronous, and that we are cause in the matter of our results – we source our results and draw to us what we want, purposely or by default. I believe that we are co-creators, and no one owns any ideas – because they're each gifts, thought energy – all ideas are gifts from the universe.

The trick is when you get an idea, you must take immediate action toward it, and only one or two steps. This is why this book can be so important –to begin to recognize, "Oh, there's another one. Oh, there's another one," and go back and think about, "Well, yes, I have wanted certain things that showed up, and I called them coincidences."

What if these were not coincidences? Just consider that. Then you get this great idea. Excited about it, most people get confused at that point. "Well, I don't know what to do. It's a great idea, but what do I do?" And when we're confused, we don't act.

The purpose of the telesummit from which this book is transcribed and edited is to make sure that everyone knows the first two easy steps to get into immediate action. What was my step? I clicked the link, and I picked up the phone and said, "Yes."

I just knew – because taking that action was against everything intellectually or environmentally or programming society-wise said, "Do not do this." And I did it anyway. I've always been an upstart.

I remember when I was a stewardess taking troops into Vietnam, living in San Francisco, not far from Janis Joplin. It was one of the most beautiful times of my life – being there in the 60s and the whole peace and freedom movement. I was blessed to be there. I was getting ready to go on a 10-day trip taking troops into Vietnam – and I messed up my checkbook. I thought I had $1,000, and I only had $100. Back then, we kept our check register by hand.

I didn't worry, I pick up the phone and called my dad. "Dad, I'm in trouble. I'm leaving tomorrow, can you help me?" I believed our life is filled with managing obstacles and I know that we can happy, healthy, and wealthy and handle the challenges, too. I expected a solution and my dad came through. I did not worry. I took a step.

We can be confident and successful – and also deal with people dying, divorcing, becoming an empty nester, losing a job. We don't have to take on the stories and the emotions of our own beliefs or those of others. In fact, that would prevent us from following our dreams.

My next immense awakening happened in 2013. I'll start however in 2008 when I began doing Think and Grow Rich Masterminds. They were all face-to-face – and they were eight to 10 weeks, meeting once a week. I went to someone's office, or they were at my house – and I had two or three programs in different places every week. I was a maniac, teaching this stuff. I didn't know why – other than it was fun and people were getting what I said, applying it and reporting back with some pretty incredible results. I was loving this work, and I had negotiated in corporate – and this is something else, for a person who is moving from corporate into entrepreneurship: You don't throw the baby out with the bathwater and quit your job.

I negotiated my last five years in corporate to work a four-day work week, Monday-Thursday. That left me Friday for personal development and evenings for Masterminds. The first year-and-a-half, I did 12 masterminds and didn't charge a penny. I believed that I had to become an expert before I could ask anyone to pay me – and they were already paying me with their time, and I continued refining my skills and writing, etc. I was in a state of deep gratitude. It was a year-and-a-half before I charged anything.

Five years later, in 2013, I was attending a woman's business luncheon. Aside: While five years had elapsed, I still had no real clue why I was teaching this crotchety 100-year-old book. The book is three times as big as it ought to be, or it could be. And it wasn't easy to understand. It wasn't exciting. So I didn't know why I was teaching this — just that I loved it, and I kept doing it. I was one of the few in my class in 2008 that never stopped — and earned back my initial investment. Most everybody gave up on their dream. Now my work is all about honing your awareness, if you will, to follow through on your dreams —how to do it, and why to do it. And what is necessary to achieve results with some consistency.

At that luncheon, the head of the North Carolina Council for Women, Beth Briggs shared that she had commissioned a report from the IWPR: Institute for Women's Policy Research in Washington, DC, on behalf of the State of North Carolina, discovering and researching the economic status of women in North Carolina — across the board. When she read the executive summary and uttered these words, "It will be 2054 before the wage gap closes in our State," I got this overwhelming 'awakening!' I had a matching physical sensation to those words. I felt warmth in my heart. I felt chills on my arms. And I was able to see, "This was the answer to my question, 'Why had I been teaching these concepts ad nauseum and writing about them for five years .' There was my Why, my specific and definite purpose.

At that moment, I realized that women did not have one clue about the principles of success in business and certainly did not know how to apply them. Why would they? We'd only been in business for a few decades. Our skills were different. They were more managing and nurturing and making sure that everybody comes in on time. Business was different, with a whole unique set of skills. I knew, "Oh, my God. THIS is why I'm here. This is why I'm an expert in this because now I can go teach women what they never knew to begin with."

My first step was to change my mastermind groups to serve only women. There weren't a lot of men anyway, and everybody was getting results – but that was my first step. Next, I created new offerings, had workshops, and began to fill my new women's high-performance mastermind. And that was 21 quarters ago.

You can the two specific steps I took. It's critical that you know the steps as soon as you get that great idea because you have to keep that idea alive and blooming for months – sometimes even years. However, now I know from my clients exactly what they need for them to do this – and that's precisely what they do every quarter. They set one important goal, and for my clients who are willing to do the work, extraordinary results are an everyday experience.

Over the past 10 years, I've created the 8 Essentials of Performance and Achievement personal development program, and now I'm licensing it to those who want to help their clients to reach the results they want – also as a side hustle and a good way to keep tabs on their clients.

I have learned that confidence is a muscle that grows in direct proportion to its use. The way we exercise that muscle, is by achieving tasks, goals, purposes, or intentions – with consistency, in spaced intervals over time. Consider your multiplication tables, when you were a kid, you practiced those tables every day or every other day for months – until to this day, if I say, "6x7" – almost everyone immediately blurts out 42.

You have perfect faith in that knowledge; that answer. That's how we learn. What I discovered over the past ten years is that achievement is not taught in public school or university. We never learned how to set a goal, what are the benchmarks for setting effective goals, what are the things you do, and you don't do.

Look at what we do with weight, exercise and health clubs. In January after you've made your new year's resolution, you are in the health club. You are tapping your foot thinking, "I've got better things to do." You're waiting for a machine or someone to help you.

February, you walk in, you can hop right on a machine. There are people on either side of you; you have lovely conversations. In March, it's a desert. Then you start again, the next January.

So it became obvious to me that people just were clueless about the how to set goals that they would achieve consistently. Once you know the benchmarks, you now have your best shot at achieving what you want. My recommendation is to set one goal per quarter. So think about that: Over the last five years and 20 business quarters, that would mean that a client would have achieved 20 distinct business goals. Particularly for women, we love (and are wired) to do a lot of things at once. What I've learned from my clients is that focusing one goal every quarter works better, because you need to get the focused purpose and the desire behind it – so that you don't give up three weeks in – which is what most people do.

Knowing the benchmarks or rules for achievement allows you to set goals that you will achieve. That's how we build confidence. We have to do the practice, the calf raises. But if you have no clue what are the common denominators to hit your goals or tasks or intentions or purposes – with consistency – you can't build confidence. You'll notice that I use goals and intentions and tasks and purposes in the same breath. Yes, there's a distinction between them. But the principles of success – and what it takes to achieve what you want – work with a task that takes this week, a goal that takes you three months, or a philanthropic goal that takes you three years. It doesn't matter. The principles are applied in the same way.

My two awakenings: One was that errant email – and I don't recommend that, unless your intuition is powerful – you've been asking a question, something shows up, you act on it. I'm told I need $16,000; I have $500. I suspect most people would say, "Well, that's not happening." Remember though the two-year-old in you who is going for the cookie. They'll pull a chair and climb up. And so, I told the universe, "This is what I'm doing. I'm going there. I've got five months. That money is coming to me." And so, it did.

The second awakening occurred five years into teaching this material and writing about it. Then, I hear the words "2054 before the wage gap closes." And instantly, I saw my great-grandchildren trying to serve me macaroni and cheese for lunch. Well, by the time I'm over 100, I would like bacon-wrapped scallops, not macaroni and cheese.

I knew that I was the one. I had trained and become an expert, to guide others to step into their infinite potential.

Download Leslie's Gift HERE:
3secrets.securechkout.com

LESLIE FLOWERS BIOGRAPHY

Leslie Flowers is a certified speaker coach and business consultant since 2008 devoting the last ten years of her twenty year personal development career with a burning mission to help women crush the wage gap 30 years earlier than predicted ... by 2025, by teaching them to "ask for what they deserve ... and be paid!"

Retiring from a 45-year career in Corporate and working 20 years in personal development, in 2008 she began studying and teaching the all time classic Think and Grow Rich. Since then she has accrued more than 14,000 hours teaching and facilitating seminars and workshops and mastermind studies, using her unique ability to articulate complex concepts in simple, 21st century terms.

In 2014 her book Champion, became an Amazon Best seller in women and business and Leslie refers to it as "the unofficial Think and Grow Rich for Women" as it outlines the high points in bullet points so it is more easy to understand and apply.

Subject matter expert in performance, achievement and mastermind, Leslie created Excelerate Experience Events in 2016 to help women (and a few smart men) learn the skills required to be successful in business.

Her mastermind program, now entering its 20th consecutive business quarter, the 8 Essentials of Performance and Achievement includes a 'train the trainer' program with licensing and certification available to those who wish to use her turnkey mastermind program to help other women grow themselves and their businesses by stepping fearlessly into their unique and infinite potential.

Leslie lives close to her children and grandchildren and refers to herself as a NanaPreneur and an UberNana, enjoying the magical combination of living a life, FINALLY, by design!

GILLIAN FOUNTAIN

THE CONCEPT OF social media came to my attention when my teenagers started talking about Facebook – and for me, Facebook wasn't really right for me; I didn't feel that I could get any business from Facebook.

I questioned whether I'd get any business online at all. Several things happened along the way to make me start to look into online social media, in particular, LinkedIn.

One very strange thing happened. An awakening moment. I was used to traditional newspaper marketing and advertising. The investment was about 500 pounds per go. One day, about two weeks after an edition had gone out, a lady phoned me and said she'd been cleaning out her rabbit hutch – and happened to see a clean part which revealed my advertisement. And I thought, "I'd just paid 500 pounds for this!"

She'd used my ad to line her rabbit hutch and was still able to read it. "I've been cleaning out my rabbit hutch, and I came across the newspaper with your advert in." I was pleased – she was a lovely lady, yet I do remember thinking, "I've just paid 500 pounds for that advert. I've got to do something different about the way I market my business."

At that time I noticed people, buyers, and suppliers asking, "What do you think about LinkedIn Local Business Platform? We don't know; we don't know how to cope with it. We don't understand it at all. What do you think about it." So, I went online and had a look. It didn't do anything for me. I was quite scared about putting myself out there online. I was used to dealing locally — and all of a sudden, this was such a global thing, where I was contacting not 1,000 people, but my brain couldn't get over tens of thousands of people. And we all know it's much bigger than that.

I felt completely unsure of myself. I was nervous as I set up my account, which sat for months without my doing anything with it. I just kept dipping in and back out again — saying, "No, I can't do it. I really can't." I didn't feel as if I had anything to say, which is silly, because I knew my business back to front. And I'd been doing it for a long time. I knew what I was talking about — yet, I still lacked that confidence.

Today I mentioned to friends and clients I was going to be part of this telesummit and they said, "What are you talking about?" I said, "Well, I'm going to talk about LinkedIn." They said, "We just don't understand it yet."

I asked if they had an account and they said, "Oh yeah, we've got an account, but I think I made it up about two years ago, and we just don't know how to use it to make the best out of it." I have had clients, highly skilled, lovely people who have got fantastic businesses — and they haven't got a good profile posted on their account. They don't want to go there because they're worried that they will make a fool of themselves, just like I was at the very beginning; I felt that nervous about putting myself out there.

I knew I had to do something so I went ahead and Step 1 for me was populating my profile — I added all my bits and pieces, ticked all the boxes, and got to the point where I thought, "Well, actually, I've done everything I can do except actually starting to use it for selling or connecting with people."

Step 2 was coming up with a plan. I would follow people who had vast numbers of followers, so I could hide in amongst all the noise that goes on. I noticed Bill Gates and Richard Branson popped up a lot, so I began watching them and commenting very low key. "Thanks for the post. That's interesting," not very much at all – gradually growing my confidence in looking at the comments and copying four or five words out, and then adding a little bit extra. Because I thought, "Well, you know, if I could add a little bit of value to the comments, at least I'd be getting somewhere." Baby steps.

One particular day, I'd been doing a charity project. Richard Branson's team had put up something about employment, and I asked the question, "Did they think that companies benefited from treating their staff well? What were the benefits they could see from treating their staff well?"

I scrolled through all the comments the day after, no response. No one had even liked my comment. And I thought, "Oh, crikey. That was a waste of time." Then, a couple of days later, up popped an article, and it addressed my questions precisely! Branson's team answered all my questions in a full article – so I was ecstatic because I just felt that this reaffirmed my belief that maybe I did know what I was talking about.

Branson's team didn't say, "Gillian Fountain, thank you very much." But they'd written an article covering the exact questions I'd asked – to the point I scrolled back through my comments to make sure that I wasn't dreaming. I was absolutely over the moon. The feeling it gave me – I don't think they realize how important it can be – and how it can make you feel. The fact was that somebody – on the team of a really big and famous company – but somebody had acknowledged that what I'd put out there was worth taking the time to write an article about. I took parts out of the article they'd written, and I included that in the marketing materials I was doing for the charity.

That feeling has never gone away ... it was a significant awakening moment for me.

If I can get the attention of somebody like that — and if they're good enough to comment on or put an article on something that I'd written — then was I going to make a fool of myself? Did I — no, I didn't. I was going to be okay on LinkedIn. After that, I had no problems at all — because it just gave me that real confidence boost.

Right after that, I started commenting on other people's articles. I stopped limiting myself to three well-known people. I still do that: If I see somebody, and they've made a comment —, and nobody's liked their post, and nobody's commented on their post — I actively go in, read whatever they've written, and put something encouraging as a comment for them. I knew how I felt — and if I can make somebody else feel like that, then that's great.

I gradually became more and more confident in what I was doing on social media. I looked at all different ways of bringing added value to other people's posts and then started writing my articles, but it didn't come overnight. It is something that I built on.

It's helped me to no end in different areas of my business and lots of other ways. People do expect you to be on LinkedIn. I've found — for instance; there was one particular instance where I linked up with a guy we both thought would be beneficial for us to meet. We thought we could do business together. He said, "Well, I'll meet you in the local hotel." Because he had is profile and photo up, off I went to the hotel. I recognized him instantly. I didn't walk into a bar thinking, "Who on earth am I meeting?" I'd already looked him up on LinkedIn. There are lots of benefits other than commenting and gathering followers. You are not only gathering your followers and connections, you start doing business. You're not selling at people because people are getting to know you — just by the way you comment and support people, then slowly the business starts rolling in.

I teach LinkedIn to my clients if they're really struggling the same as I did — and quite often, it is the ladies. I do teach them how to do it — or I do it for them. They're more interested in finding out the mechanics of it, and how you can gather connections and build up your following. Because obviously, they want to do the same sort of thing. And it does give you the credibility and the recognition in your industry.

Although there is much competition on LinkedIn, you've all got your individual ways of doing things and your experiences that you've gained along the way. So your personality does shine through. It's been very good in that sense because I've trained people on how to use LinkedIn effectively and how to make the best out of their profile.

Last year that I started seeing posts about LinkedIn Local – taking business connections online, and meet them offline. I co-host LinkedIn Local for Basingstoke. LinkedIn Local is growing at a rate of knots across the globe. It's gone from nothing – absolutely nothing – to being in many, many countries. And it's bringing a lot of people together offline.

The beauty of that is we are seeing people that wouldn't comment on LinkedIn but had an account, were coming along to see what was going on.

Almost before my eyes, their online character changes – and they're all commenting on LinkedIn. So by doing little things builds confidence all the time.

People do take you more seriously when you are on LinkedIn. Even for entrepreneurs and small business owners, who write and post differently. It's more informative. There's a great deal of learning and expertise on LinkedIn. There are also opportunities to collaborate with people and share ideas. These are not the Facebook-type of comments or posts. You get corporate people primarily on LinkedIn. There are also small businesses owners and entrepreneurs providing value and at the same time, gathering new connections. It is a great platform for learning and engaging with other people. I was contacted on LinkedIn by a university to do business with them. I also connected with a construction worker. So we've gone from a one-man band from a college – and it's just staggering, the expanse of experience that is on LinkedIn and how much it can grow.

I spent probably far too long observing all the different people. I was also wary about it. I didn't really want to connect with people that would be controversial or negative. So I was very careful with whom I connected.

I chose my times and watched what was going on. I recommend when you first begin on social media, that you sit back and see with whom you relate initially. There are areas and comments on social media that I avoid, yet at the same time, I know that I learn – every time I go onto social media.

Download Gillian's Gift HERE:
http://38partnership.co.uk/excelerate.html

GILLIAN FOUNTAIN BIOGRAPHY

Gillian Fountain never thought, when I became a business owner nearly 3 decades ago, she would still be running her own business all these years later. HEr business started years before social media and the cloud.

My business is 38 Partnership, a Brand Management and Marketing Company and Gillian helps business owners promote their products and services. In the beginning, her main aim was to just sell product and help Brands introduce and take their product to market. As the company grew, she became International Distributors, importing and exporting. working with warehousing and distribution, at exhibitions, even helping to design product and packaging. We sold products to the independents, high street stores such as Harrods and John Lewis, tourist attractions, even Castles.

Today Gillian works closely with business owners who want to push ahead with their businesses, really see how far they can go, what they can achieve, looking at solutions to get them to the next level or fathom out why they are standing still. This often involves re-vamping websites, creating bespoke graphics and helping with the ever-changing world of social media.

Gillian is Currently producing material for college students to give them a better understanding of real-life marketing.

Launched #Linkedinlocal #Basingstoke, helping people on LinkedIn meet their connections made online, to meet offline with the aim of firming up and building stronger business relationships.

KATIE GAILES

I'VE ALWAYS HAD a great relationship with books, perhaps because they were not completely accessible when I was growing up. I had to walk to the library to use the books there and to do my homework. One of the first things I did when I started my professional career and had some money was to buy a set of the Encyclopedia Britannica. I also joined every book club! I have always had this thing about books and wanted to hold them in my hands. It wasn't unusual for me to see an interesting book and pick it up and start reading it. Or sometimes, I'd pick it up just because I wanted to have it. I've always been a reader.

It was 1992 when I was 12 when I remember walking through Sam's Club and saw this big table of books — all in stacks. There was one book that caught my eye. It was a paperback and cost $6.95, so it could be an impulse buy. I picked up, took it home, and soon I cracked it open and started reading it.

At another time in my life, I had moved to another State, had unofficially adopted a 14-year-old family member, and she was living with me. I was going through a divorce and had changed jobs. A lot was going on. I might've pushed my ex-husband down the step for a penny or less. So a lot of emotional turmoil, a lot of uncertainty, a lot of change, and a lot of stress made up my environment. I started reading through this book – and I got to a point in the book where the author was explaining the concepts about personal responsibility and accountability. There was a diagram there. And I went back and I re-read that part, and I looked at the diagram again. And I thought, "Oh, my." That challenged my whole view of where I was in life at that time – at what my role was and getting me to that point – and how I could move forward. You know how you feel when you get this awakening chill? It's when a part of your body goes to sleep – and then, suddenly, the blood starts rushing back in it. And you feel all this tingling, tingling, tingling. I felt that. And I said to myself, "I can't just read this book. I have to study this book." That book was Covey's 7 Habits of Highly Effective People. The diagram that caught my attention was the circle of influence vs. the circle of concern.

Sometimes we feel angry because we're not accepting any responsibility for where we are. We can be innocent, but not guilt-free in certain situations. Then I was compelled to stop reading and go back to the very beginning of that book – and start taking notes as I went through and read a chapter and then letting the information marinate and then acting on it. It changed the way that I saw what had happened in my relationship with my husband, in my career – and what my responsibility was for myself moving forward.

I kept that book by my side wherever I went. It took me a little bit longer to read it because I wasn't just reading it. I was studying it. That book became my mentor, and I shared that book and the concepts from that book with my ex-husband – whom I stopped calling my ex-husband. I just called him "Maggie's Dad." What mattered was not anything that happened between us in the past. What mattered was that we had to co-parent this child. That changed my whole paradigm. It changed the way that we interacted with each other. And I think moving forward; we may have had only two arguments. We got a divorce without a judge telling us what to do. We settled everything without fighting over anything – and that book, it became my mentor.

In fact, I believe in it so much, I've given probably seven or eight copies of that book to others as gifts – and said, "Don't read this book. Just study it."

That was my awakening and the first time that I realized how powerful books could be as mentors. And let me tell you: Sometimes, you get started down a path, and you fall off the wagon. Mama would call that "backsliding." Mama was a preacher, so she used those words. And that book, you pick it back up again – and re-read, and refresh – and you're back on track. So it's like the mentor that you have right on your night table or your bookshelf or in your purse – that you can always go back to when you need a refresher. When you need to be renewed.

As I reread this book, I did find new applications or new areas in my life where I did not apply that because it wasn't apparent to me at the time.

Since that book, I've gone out and found other books that served as my mentors.

This awakening also changed the way I look at possessing books. So having a book – especially a personal development or a self-help book – to me became more of a significant thing. I looked at them as a tool. I used to belong to book clubs where you get six books every month. And if you didn't send them back, you paid for them. That was before we started doing everything online. I stopped those book clubs because I didn't want to read all those books that somebody else picked out for me. I wanted to be much more deliberate in my reading.

On any given day, you will find me usually with a book in my bag.

Since that experience, I have found other books, I said, "Ooh, I wish I'd read this one first."

I compiled a list of six books in the order in which I recommend they be read I read them all together and some recommendations to make time for reading.

You don't have to change your life all around to do this. Just takes a few minutes a day. And start with the idea in mind that you're not just reading the book – you're studying the book. You're getting involved with the book. You're there to learn, and your mind is open – and you're going to be deliberate. You're not going to rush.

Awakening your infinite potential is a journey and you know it's out there. It's infinite. You are on this beautiful journey toward infinity. And who knows what exciting things are out there in the future? I've found with books as mentors, they're always available to you – and at the point where you need a refresher, you want to go back and grab one. Or you want to add one – because this new one is now the right one on your journey – they're always there. They don't replace physical, actual human mentors that you would interact with – but they're another essential part of your arsenal that you can use to take you toward your infinite potential.

Download Katie's Gift HERE:
https://mailchi.mp/51a0c555c514/book-mentorship-guide

KATIE GAILES BIOGRAPHY

Katie Gailes has been called a 'force of nature' because of her creativity and energy.

After a long corporate career, Katie started a consulting practice that she ran full-time for six years. She then assumed several counseling, consulting, and program management roles with other organizations that serve small business owners and entrepreneurs. Katie is a 2018 Triangle Business Journal Women in Business award recipient, a HUB Collaborative Partner award recipient, and also received a Paul Harris Fellow Award from Rotary International and the Rotary Foundation.

An avid reader, her creative outlets are gardening and writing. She has found mentors for her personal passions and her professional aspirations in books. Katie wants to use her passion for writing and reading to show others how to do the same.

HALEY GRAY

I AM EXCITED to share my awakening of my infinite potential. Many times people look at where I am now, especially with the Women's Entrepreneur Network group on Facebook, and professionally, and they think, "Oh, she's just got it. This is easy peasy, lemon squeezy for her." It hasn't always been that way. I am a computer programmer by training, and if you know anything about programmers, you know that we are not typically extroverts. I was a programmer for many years in my career and wanted more. I always had the goal and the vision that I could move myself up the corporate ladder yet I kept having kids! I found myself pregnant, babies, and more babies – and not able to move where I wanted to go in my career. I was frustrated by the whole thing.

I felt I was dying a bit on the inside every day when I went to work. I was following someone else's rules constantly. When I realized this, I began figuring out where I was going from there. I knew from a young age that I ultimately wanted to get my MBA, so I signed up for my MBA at Duke. My husband was surprisingly supportive of the whole process. While I was there the shutters on my eyes started coming off. My managers at my corporate job kept telling me that I was going to leave, and I would repeat, "No, I'm not. I'm going to be here the whole time." I had no intention of leaving – so it was "No, I'm going to be here in my corporate job forever. I'm going to grow; I'm going to move into more leadership roles, move my way up the food chain and keep going that way."

While it wasn't, "Hey, I'm going to leave." It became like little drops of awareness – where I started saying, "Huh, there's more out there. There's more that can be done." I began looking around and seeing what my opportunities were. Just a little bit here and a little bit there – it wasn't like, any great big ta-dah kind of a thing. Little, teeny, tiny cracks – and I could see sunlight coming through. People would approach me while I was in the MBA program along with friends in small business saying, "So, you're getting your MBA at Duke. Here, can you run through my numbers and tell me what it is exactly what I need to do here? Should I buy that new storefront? Should I do this? Should I do that? Should I do the other?"

That was the point where I discovered a passion for helping small business owners figure out what they were going to do to grow their business. Helping them problem-solve and figuring out the right solutions that worked for them – not what they thought they should do, but to go digging at a deeper level – and figure out, "Okay, so here's what you think you should do. But what if we look at all of the possibilities and think outside of the proverbial just a bit – and ignore the fact that maybe there's a box – and consider all of the alternatives?"

I had one friend ask, "Should I go buy this plot of land here and build a store, and we're going to have to grow our revenue 40% just to accommodate this?" We took a step back, and ultimately they ended up deciding to close their storefront and do service calls only. They reduced the number of employees and increased the amount of money in their pocket at the end of the day, reducing their stress levels. So sometimes, it's "Oh, good, you can find another solution that may not be obvious." That was a first big win for me –it was exciting. I was thrilled by getting to see their results. "Okay, so I'm helping my clients get outstanding results – that are maybe not even what they dreamed that they could do – maybe even better than they thought, with options that they didn't even realize that they had. They're making more money, working fewer hours, have less stress, and are getting what they wanted in life."

It became addictive to me; somebody who had been an engineer. And while yes, engineering is about problem-solving, it doesn't affect people's lives and make a difference. That was that point, for me, "Oh, you mean I can get to help people and get paid for this?"

I took a few first steps once I figured this out. I made sure that I got my entrepreneurship and innovation concentration while at Duke. I took as many classes as I could. I was already there. I was in the middle of the program and started meeting other people who were starting their businesses. I was asking a lot of questions, and working through that whole process of, "Okay, so what does it look like for me to do this?" I also started blogging and trying different things out, talking to other people who had blogs and who had websites so that I could begin to understand what all of the pieces were that I needed to look at – not just from an academic perspective. It's always such a thimbleful compared to what you're going to have to learn – because you can only learn so much in such a short period of time. I enjoyed getting to know other entrepreneurs who were facing a lot of the same challenges that I was. Or who maybe were ahead of me – and who had a lot of really valuable advice.

After a while I found Becky Dickson's group and other entrepreneurial groups online. Those gave me a lot of insight into the coaching industry – and then I discovered Marie Foreleo. I found Kendrick Shope – many different coaches, and I started looking and reading and going through this whole process of learning more and more. As I was finishing my MBA program, I was deciding on my exit strategy from corporate, and working through my concentration, trying to absorb all of the pieces that I needed to learn while I was in my concentration. Putting together my first business plan for my own business was exciting and terrifying, and there was so much research to do.

The most important thing I did for me was stopping and listening to myself — and to my gut, saying, "Okay, so what do I think I need to do next?" Given the analytics piece, the emotional piece, and the financial pieces — and considering the context of my life at the time, I needed to think about all of that. Think deeply about where I was going and what pieces I needed next — and finding people and resources. Step 1 Pay attention, Step 2 Start looking for the right resources.

If you are a bit shy about the inner work, I would recommend working on expanding your friend network first. So many times, when we're in corporate America, our family and our friends are our families and our friends, but they're not necessarily the people that are going to buy from us.

I've seen a lot of people become frustrated because their family and their friends don't buy from them — whether it's direct sales or a storefront — they're heartbroken because they don't feel supported. It feels awful when your family and friends say, "I'm going to buy this Coach handbag, but I'm not going to buy one of your handmade creations from you." They don't see that as being any problem — and of course, you as the person who is making those handbags feel that slight and that emotional cut. It's almost like being sliced to death a thousand times — death by a million small cuts.

So finding that support network, those friends who can support you in your business. Whatever you're looking to do — find a core group of people and friends who are friends, who are going to help you make that transition and who will be there when you need somebody to rely and lean on. As you're making changes in your life, there are going to be people in your old life who are negatively triggered by the transitions you begin making. It may be your spouse; it may be your mother. You may get really weird comments — even from your children — about, "Mom, why are you doing this?"

I would recommend when beginning to create your network of friends is having conversations. Respond to other people's posts. Get to know people. The biggest mistake I see people making in business and life is that they rush too fast into the whole "me first" thing – rather than observing and interacting and contributing before they get back. The more you contribute, and you put out there and start reaching toward other people, having coffee with them virtually or in person, and connecting with people, the faster that energy comes flowing back to you. The more that you focus on "me, me, me, me, me" – whether it's in a mom's group, or a networking group, or business, the faster people are going to run from you, and you're going to be chasing them, wondering why nobody wants anything to do with you.

Awakening your infinite potential is an interesting concept. It's not an external thing. It's very much internal; very much a profound awakening and a discovery about who you are or who you might be in that next phase of your life. And knowing that the only constant is change.

We are continually changing, the cells of our body are changing, and the person we are is changing. Being aware of that and starting to be mindful of how much amazing, pure brilliance we're truly capable of, you really can create brilliant things.

That person who asked me when I was doing my MBA "Hey, can you help me run these numbers and tell me, should I do this or should I do that in my business?" triggered my awakening. It was inspiring to me that ultimately, what I helped them with was what they ended up deciding to do. That just lit up my world in a whole different way than being a software engineer ever had – because I got to make a difference.

Juggling –this is a different kind of excitement, isn't it?

It was a different kind of excitement than raising a family and a different type of energy. My brain is wired to get high on helping others. Maybe yours is that way too.

When we help people help themselves, it produces a whole other level of excitement. Helping people figure out how to best market their business that makes sense to them lights up all of the pleasure centers in my brain! When I discovered that, I was amazed, and fell in love with what I was doing.

My gift to the readers below is a checklist for new entrepreneurs, and I share the things no one ever tells you. It's the stuff I wish someone had told me when I first started and it's information that is not generally available.

I think it's important to recognize that we have access to our infinite potential within us. We have to have faith in that and that we can take charge and do it for ourselves.

Download Haley's Gift HERE:
nittygrittylanding.pages.ontraport.net

HALEY GRAY BIOGRAPHY

Haley Lynn Gray founded Leadership Girl with the radical notion that women can harness their unique power and skills to become highly effective leaders.

Best-selling author of Leadership Girl, and graduate of Duke's Fuqua School of Business with an MBA with a concentration in entrepreneurship and Innovation, Haley has experience with starting up successful small businesses, growing them, then selling them.

Haley has worked with hundreds of small business owners since Leadership Girl was founded. She has a passion for helping their owners find ways to grow their business, acquire visibility, and transform into the go-to expert in their industry, while saving them significant amounts of money.

She is also the founder of the 60,000 strong Women's Entrepreneur Network Group on Facebook, which she successfully grew in two years. It is recognized as one of the best, most engaging, and helpful groups of this type on Facebook.

CHRYSTAL HARRIS

I AM A woman in the medical field; a medical doctor. As one of my mentors used to say, "Always a physician, but not only a physician." Thus, I am also many other things. Two of my favorites are mother and coach. As a physician, I once lost sight of my potential, and couldn't see my way to doing all the things that I loved and wanted to do. I was struggling and stuck, and maybe at times, you've felt that way, too.

Thankfully, I had a moment that awakened me and changed my life. And so as you read this chapter, my intention is for you learn about how I awoke to my potential and gained more energy, more time, and more fulfillment – and to discover how it can help you to realize your full potential.

Since I was very young, I dreamed of being a doctor. When I was about four, my grandfather had become very sick with what I later found out was emphysema. And my mother and three of her sisters took care of him in his final years. I thought it was fantastic how these women worked together to take care of his needs and to keep him in good spirits. I imagined being able to take care of people just as they had done – and to keep them in good spirits as well. As the years went by, I was very good in science and math, and I imagined how doctoring would allow me to help people, to support my family, and to be a great mother – just like my mom was. I held onto this dream all through childhood. When I graduated school as a young adult, I thought I had a free ride. Because for me, that was the hard part. You see, I'd given up romantic relationships, family time, and personal time. I'd also missed the weddings of friends, graduations, and funerals of loved ones. For me, I felt like I had earned it through my sacrifice.

Even at the time of graduation, I started to feel a little tugging in my heart, because maybe that wasn't the right way to go about it. I was already feeling some bitterness for what I had given up.

I was working with a great family medicine team – and my colleagues were amazing providers, skilled and supportive. Plus, I loved my patients. The problem was, I wasn't enjoying medicine like I thought I would. It wasn't too hard, but it was harder and harder to get through each day. It was because I was living with regrets. My energy level was low, and I felt less fulfilled each day. I realized that I had burned out, and I was wondering, "Was there something to fill that missing piece?"

Well, I felt very alone. And it turns out that studies show that about 40% of physicians experience some burnout, about 15% report some form of depression and almost 50% of women in medicine report having burned out at some point during their careers.

So I wasn't alone. And maybe the reader has experienced some of this burnout, too, because this is not unique to the medical profession. Still, I felt guilty about not loving my chosen profession. I mean, who doesn't want to help people? Sometimes I even felt like I was ungrateful and that I didn't deserve to be happy. I'd gotten to the point where I couldn't even imagine bringing kids into my life. That's the one thing that weighed heavily on me. Then, in less than a year, I lost two of my family medicine colleagues to cancer.

Two friends that I'd gone to medical school with. They had both been ill while we were at school – but both of them had gone into remission. And then, while out in practice, both of their cancers came back with a vengeance. Since they had these conditions for a while, they lived their lives to the fullest. They did what they loved – which was practice medicine. I remember them coming to the office wearing face masks. Sometimes they would have IV bags hanging – or even, they would come in riding motorized wheelchairs.

And they always did it with a smile. That's because medicine was their passion. It was their passion that gave them energy and fulfillment. While my friends were living with cancer, I knew that I needed to find my passion the way they did – because that's what I needed as well. I learned an amazing lesson from them: that our hard work wasn't about being a doctor. It was about the opportunity to live our passion without regrets. That's exactly what they did. That's what I wanted to do, too. So I stopped thinking about what I was going to do and started thinking about why I wanted to do it. I wanted to be able to take care of my family, help people in my community, and be a happy, healthy mother taking care of business – just like my mom did. None of those things required me living with regret. I decided then and there that I would do what it took to care of myself inside and out.

Usually, I'm nervous about change – because change can be hard. Other people are like that, too. But this time when I made that decision that I could do all the things I wanted to do, it just felt like a weight was lifted off of me. I felt really easy – like I had made the right choice. I was once in darkness, and here I was in the light. And it was almost instantaneous. If I could only tell you one thing it would be this: That night, I slept well for the first time in years. Not only that, things began to show up to help me along the way. People began to show up. And I also mentioned that during that time is when I met Leslie Flowers and I was starting to build my support systems – and I started living on my terms.

I also stopped worrying so much about what others thought of me. I transitioned from the practice of medicine to teaching it. I then opened up a business, Crystal Violet Solutions, to coach others through their life transitions and stressors. I also had a baby. And that was the biggest joy of my life, having my son. I began working from home, and I loved what I did. I loved being a mom. I was the happiest I've ever been in my life. My life had more meaning and more fulfillment.

A couple of years into that, my son was about two years ago, I started to get that little feeling again. I couldn't believe it! How does someone who's so happy start getting that little nagging feeling? I tried to ignore it, but I knew that that wasn't going to cut it. Then I thought I needed to do more with my business, maybe. And so I tried to do it on my own. I started doing some online marketing and watching some videos here and there and learning a few things. But nothing felt right, and I wasn't building any momentum. It just really felt forced. I knew I needed to get some help.

That's when I reached out to someone who I knew could probably take me to that next level. My amazing, accomplished business coach Leslie Flowers. I spoke with her about wanting to do more to help others. I told her that I didn't know what it is that I was supposed to do. She reminded me that there are no coincidences – and to be aware of things showing up in my life.

A few days after I talked to Leslie, I saw an article entitled, "Women are now a majority of entering medical students nationwide." And that's when I had my Awakening. It was like a light switch came on. I knew my path! Everything that I had done – all the things that I went through – actually were leading up to this very point. I thought about how in four years we will graduate more female doctors than male doctors. I also thought about the struggles that I had and realized: It is up to us – those who have walked that path – to make sure that these females enter a culture of medicine that is more supportive of women living into their full potential.

My awakening came with an idea of women being the change that they wanted to see. We're not only about supporting women but living the lives that we would like to see them live as well. Unfortunately, the culture of medicine doesn't always support that.

Reflection. Interaction with a male attending physician.

I was an intern working off-service, and I had been working in the office for a few weeks. The attending was reading the newspaper when I came in, and he remarked that a local, older female physician had passed away. I glanced at the newspaper and saw this lengthy article about this female physician who had a bright career, amazing service to the community – all the things that a young doctor would want to emulate. Then the attending physician said out to the group, "Now, she knew how to be a good lady doctor. She never got married, and she never had any kids." I was stunned, but I didn't say anything. And no one else said anything either. Statements like that have no place in any profession – yet, with our silence, we had agreed with him. So I want to do my part now to make that change in the culture of medicine.

I am aware that only 3% of people are happy, healthy, and wealthy in the world. Less than 1% of those women and even fewer of those are women in the medical field. It's time to make that change as well. Thus, WISE Women was born. WISE Women stands for Women In Scrubs Elevating Women. And the mission is for females in medicine – and in fields that are also medicine-adjacent – to come together for a common cause. The mission of WISE Women is to support the efforts of women in the medical field to obtain a high quality of life and realize their full potential. To be examples for our rising medical colleagues, so they know they, too, can do all things. To change the culture of medicine to empower women in all their roles.

I recognize this is a tall order. And I also know that my infinite potential allows for something like this to be realized. I also recognize that only by helping others to realize their infinite potential will we be able to make a difference. I know it can be done. WISE Women is not only about elevating women, but about elevating our communities and our cultures to their full potential as well. I look forward to that – and I'm working hard to build up that group.

I recognized my awakening because I had this feeling of – this kind of glow that came from down deep. Before I had this kind of nagging feeling – and then, this was like, a warmth inside. It made me realize that if I had had something like this earlier, then some of that burnout, some of that feeling of being alone wouldn't have been there – and I could've been a little more productive. I probably also would have left sooner – and I wouldn't have lost some of that time in my life where I sacrificed things that were so important to me.

This is really about following your passion. And my passion, as I've grown, is about supporting people who are in the medical field through their different roles. And so, there are going to be some folks who are coming up and going into medicine as well as those already in the profession.

There are going to be some people who are going into other fields but support medical professionals or support what medical professionals are doing. It's about helping all of those people do the things that they enjoy doing – and to fulfill their passion.

Because it's about everyone awakening to their infinite potential, one of the things that I wanted to stress is listening to your instinct. Once I started listening to my intuition and that gnawing, nagging feeling in the pit of my belly, or this warm glow that tells you, "This is it." Or it could kind of feeling stuck and not sure where to go – the ultimate message is that there needs to be a change. It's telling you, it's time to awaken to your next level. Taking the first step is essential. For me, it was refocusing on my purpose and then being alert to where it was leading me. For others, it could be – like we said, going into the medical field. It could be building a new business, starting a new relationship. Most important, however, is listening to your intuition.

My gift below is an achievement assessment to help you determine your achievement style and to help evaluate your starting point.

Download Chrystal's Gift HERE:
https://crystalviolet.sendlane.com/view/full-potential-blueprint

CHRYSTAL HARRIS MD BIOGRAPHY

Chrystal B. Harris MD is a physician, medical educator, coach, and a mother. This North Carolina native has strong roots in the Tarheel state. She grew up in Raleigh, then headed to Winston-Salem graduating from Wake Forest University with a Bachelor's in Biology, and attended the Brody School of Medicine in eastern NC where she obtained her Doctorate in Medicine. Chrystal did her training in family medicine and saw a variety of patients in practice as well as taught medicine in the classroom.

Through her own experiences and working with patients, students, and other medical professionals, she saw how the struggle to reach personal, health, and professional goals can be overwhelming and frustrating, but it didn't have to be. With this in mind, she transitioned from the practice of medicine to coaching individuals on ways to make a faster, smoother transition from dreaming of something better to living that dream. Thus, her company Crystal Violet Solutions was born.

Believing the mantra "Always a physician but not only a physician," her mission involves working with women in medicine to create a lifestyle that matches their vision and to connect them with the people, places, and things that make their lives less stressful, more manageable, and more enjoyable.

Her vision is that as the face of medicine changes to be more female that there is a change in the culture that supports women in medicine in their endeavors to be happy, healthy, wealthy, and the best providers they can be.

AIGARS KAULIŅŠ

I WAS THIRTY-TWO when I got my diagnosis of ADHD. Up until that time I was a total mess because I didn't know what's happening to me. One program was that everyone was reminding me "Some is wrong with you. You're doing something wrong, and this is how it should be done. You are too impulsive, and you can't stay focused." I was bombarded with these messages from others.

Before long I began to believe it was true and step by step it grew more and more stressful for me. I started to show signs of depression; nothing seemed to go the way I wanted it to.

I remember when I was nine, I had big dreams like most children. And here I was an adult, with a great career, earning good money and all that goes with it, and still, I felt something was wrong with me. I couldn't solve my problem.

In my late twenties, I remember walking across the street and crumbling to the pavement with a mammoth cluster headache attack. I was in pain, and I was confused. Then these cluster headaches came in cycles for the next five years.

Working with a famed neurologist on my cluster headaches, after looking at all my medical reports, looked up and said, "The reports say that you have ADHD!" Then he asked if I wanted medication for it. I was already taking 15 pills a day for cluster headaches without much result. More medicine?

When I went home that day, I began to think about taking a look at personal growth to find the answer, "What is wrong with me?" I still couldn't answer that for myself. I learned that this is common with ADHD, asking the questions, "Why it's happening to me? What is this trying to teach me?"

I did the research, googling this question: "What is the spiritual meaning of ADHD?" The very first article I read explained that this is teaching me acceptance and love. I started to look deeper for more answers. It was clear that I did not accept nor did I love myself anymore.

At that moment I understood that I didn't come into this world by accident; that there is a purpose for me. This was my awakening moment or turning point when I started to move in a different direction. When I understood I still have that power within me and a message which I can share.

I did more and more research searching for a scientific explanation as to what is ADHD while I focused on spirituality, personal growth, and lifestyle changes.

A fair explanation of what was happening to me was a clear message that I can help others with their struggle with ADHD. I believe we all come into this world with a message to share. No matter our hardship, illness, or sickness it is a preparation to bring your message to the world. The message within us could come from God, the Universe, Source, I don't know. What I do know is that others should hear it. If this story can help another, I'm happy to share it.

We grow up being programmed to believe what our parents, grandparents, and what those we love to believe. It's when we become adults that many of us find that those beliefs aren't our beliefs and have even been passed down from grandparents. Once I learned

I no longer needed to be programmed with their words, everything changed for me.

We hold these beliefs, even though we were never told about them. Once I began doing a lot of mindset work, I began to move forward and live a better life. And I found that we can still be held back if we don't actively work on our belief systems ... the ones we don't even know we have. Understanding this made my mind and thinking processes more clear. You can use meditation or binaural beats of other techniques to clean out or reprogram our subconscious mind with a new belief.

And that's made my mind or thinking process more clear, and for that you can do meditation. You can use binaural beats or – it's a lot of techniques what you can use to clean out of your subconscious mind those conditions.

If you don't recognize or accept these lessons as turning points, you can't get results for yourself or help others that perhaps you were meant to help.

Should you have ADHD or the symptoms of the disease, don't talk about it and think about it. Focus your mind on the strength you to have and progress you are making in your life. Dwelling on ADHD will have you begin to experience those symptoms. A simple truth I have learned.

Download Aigars free Gift HERE:
https://infinitepotentialwithadhd.com/telesummit-opening-your-infinite-potential/

AIGARS KAULIŅŠ BIOGRAPHY

Aigars Kauliņš, ADHD Attention deficit hyperactivity disorder and mindset coach, is from Latvia and started his career at age 14, quick to learn leading him to move up the career ladder quite fast. A management professional by age 23, the career melted away 5 years later.

Diagnosed with cluster headaches, Aigars lost muscle tone to the point of a new born, could not control his emotions and was in chronic stress. Often angry, he almost always felt anxious and depressed. His self doubt led quickly to numerous failures and to the conclusion that he was alone and no one could help him.

Determined to find answers to the question "why is this happening to me?" And so he did. At age 32 he was relieved to be diagnosed with ADHD. His turning point or awakening moment.

SHEYENNE KREAMER

I'LL START WITH a bit of back story on my awakening. I have learned that sometimes, the things we're meant to do can be staring us in the face – and we don't realize it. So we need a little bit of a wakeup call here and there.

During my time of corporate America, I didn't realize was that I was heavily trained as a problem solver. My math and computer science degrees were all about problem-solving. I was a project manager which also was all about problem-solving. And, I became a leader and facilitator of what corporate America used to call Quality Circles, which was all about bringing teams of people together to be able to solve problems and to reduce costs for the company (one of those problems). That is a huge part of my corporate career for some time until I started experiencing multiple layoffs. Then everything began to shift for me. I found it very difficult to get a job in the area that I lived in Vermont when I got laid off. When I moved to North Carolina I got laid off again, it too it became challenging to find a job here.

For me, the problem solver, my big a-ha moment that was understanding that I could be a problem solver by becoming a business owner. That was the first piece. I learned how to become a management consultant. I also became a career coach based on all the experiences that I had going through multiple layoffs. These skills showed me more and more ways to become an even better problem solver.

But the fascinating piece was that my experience with problem-solving, initially, was mostly working in professional environments – working with unemployed professionals and working in corporate America. It wasn't until sometime later when I was out networking where I met a woman from our local Human Services – who loved hearing me talk about my concept of living your song.

Next, she invited me into her office to present about living your song to a room full of social workers. This experience was very new for me. I had never worked in Human Services or had exposure to folks who were living in low-income situations. So it was new and very unusual.

What happened next was mind-boggling. As I was getting into my presentation about my concept of living your song – I noticed all the social workers sitting forward, on the edge of their seats! They were just fascinated with what I was talking about. At that moment I had a déjà vu experience. I felt like I had been here and done this before. It was such a strong physical experience that it shook me to the core. I had to stop talking for a minute because I completely had forgotten what I was talking about!

I've never had a déjà vu experience like that, that just stopped me in my tracks. Once I regained my composure, remembered where I was, and finished my presentation, everybody was thoroughly excited and engaged – and I walked out of the room, scratching my head, asking myself, "Oh, my God. What just happened?"

I was in the space of knowing what it is I needed to be doing, yet was experiencing a little resistance to that 'knowing.' It felt like 'somebody' grabbed me by the hand and was pulling me along.

The female supervisor in the Human Services group told me that they were going to create a whole event around my concept to help those looking for work. I asked her she was targeting for this project and she said we want everybody.

Then I asked her who 'everybody' was and she was talking about professional-levels and folks who had been in the welfare system— all in one place. And I said, "Wow, I don't think that's ever been done before, has it?" And she said, "You know, you might be right. But that doesn't mean we're not going to do it."

THAT was my next step getting engaged and involved in creating this event. We called it something about balancing life and talking about creating work that you enjoyed while also having a balanced life. I found it interesting that very few people attended the event from the Human Services. I had extra time and used it to help 'solve' what had happened there and "Why did we not see some of the folks we wanted to include in this event?"

Sometime later someone suggested that I might reach out to the local community college offering the class that I had created called "Find Your Song and Sing It." Someone shared with me that once I was on staff with the college, I could take my concept into homeless shelters, working with the formerly incarcerated community and working with people that I had not worked with before. That was the beginning of opening my eyes and showing me just how much of an impact that I could make an impact at a level, something I didn't even realize was possible.

Until my awakening, I didn't understand that there was a place for me to help those who were unemployed. I talk a lot about long-term unemployed as being a sweet spot for me, yet even working with people who are short-term unemployed was good for me. But I had started down that path because I knew I had something to offer concerning helping folks in transition. Then it seemed all of a sudden, other people and opportunities things started coming my way. I was afraid, all right. I felt the fear and ... I did it anyway!

While in unfamiliar arenas, there was always that little voice in the back of my head as I am walking through fear; my mom's voice. I realized a lot of people have a song in their heart that they don't even understand is there. I kept hearing my mom's voice, who worked in all kinds of state government agencies. For eighteen years she told me she was frustrated because she didn't think the agencies were help-ing people as much as they could. Without knowing it until then, I had internalized those thoughts and those pieces of information from her. Those thoughts were sitting hidden in my subconscious for quite a long time. Something inside of me had integrated them and decided that I needed to be out there helping some of those people.

My advice is that if you keep hearing the same thing over and over from different people and people keep saying "You should consider this" or "You should think about that," and you're just shutting the ideas down as not 'part of your plan,' I invite you to explore these thoughts anyway.

I use the word "synchronicity" to explain those things that keep showing up over and over again. They all have a common thread so why not stop and say to yourself "Okay, there's something for me to learn here. There's something for me to do here that I'm not fully aware of yet." Be open to that. Once open to considering a new point of view, things will show up in some of the craziest ways.

My gift below will have you examine the question "What have you come through in your life, where there may be wisdom that you've gained and knowledge that you have that could bring hope, help, and healing to other people?" It's necessary and as you realize that what you have been through actually IS significant.

We all can be part of a very large super-puzzle that can create peace and prosperity on the planet for all. That is genuinely who I be-lieve we are — yet we're so resistant. We get so caught up in thinking, "Oh, no. That's not for me. No, I would never do that." And I was the queen of no, let me tell you. Over and over again, I would say no to things that were coming toward me.

If we can stop when we recognize we're saying no to something too many times — and allow it. Allow ourselves to be open to a new idea, and allow ourselves to explore — what you'll find in that explora-tion is your authentic self.

Download Sheyenne's Gift HERE:
http://www.iwebatool.net/0006.php?user=projectuplift

SHEYENNE KREAMER BIOGRAPHY

Sheyenne Kreamer, CEO of Triangle Solutions Alliance, Inc., focuses on helping people at all levels of society "Live Their Song". Sheyenne uses the phrase "Community & Economic Development Corporation" to describe the integrated system called TSAI. She believes that we are all "born with a song in our heart" for creating a unique gift to the world. The key to creating peace & prosperity in the world requires each of us to find that unique passion, purpose & gift, learn how to package it as a product or service, and then find others with a similar mission for group collaboration and implementation.

Sheyenne has created a variety of classes, coaching programs, and apprenticeship programs to become a one-stop resource for products and services to help individuals and groups implement their vision. Her "stepping stones for success" methodologies allow her to work with people from 8 to 80, no matter what their current income situation is.

Sheyenne's qualifications for this work include 12 years in manufacturing/project management, 6 years in recruiting & staffing, and 18 years in career transition services which include both job search & entrepreneurial strategies.

She has taught classes at UNC-Greensboro, ECPI and The Friday Center at UNC-CH, has conducted young entrepreneur summer camps, and continues to teach entrepreneurial skills at Wake Technical Community College. She is now contracted with NC State to bring the Live Your Song message to the corporate world. Her students at Wake Tech have included formerly incarcerated people and homeless women.

OLGA MONROE

I LIKE YOU have likely had several awakening moments. My most recent awakening moment was in a dark, hot, Bikram yoga studio on one particular day. There is nothing in the studio other than a mirror so for ninety minutes you are looking at yourself constantly. It is quite an awakening – not only are you looking at yourself, but you're sweating profusely in the 105-degree room. My awakening occurred during a time of my life that was about as dark and deep and desolate and confused and chaotic as I'd ever been – and frankly, it was the only place that I could get away from that.

That was in 2009. Through many twists and turns, I am happily working with a company called Ruby Ribbon. My best advice is to hold the thought "Never give away your power." I share that because for me, being in that deep, dark place is where I consciously and intentionally gave away my power.

Let's look at the power of confidence. Take a breath for a moment, and ponder what that means to you. It likely means something different for every one of us.

1. The power of confidence not only is a power in itself, but it has the power to bring us joy, satisfaction, the ability to take risks, and along with that, a paycheck. If you will compare any person, the confident one has the edge. And as women, we need that edge.

2. Women entrepreneurs start most of the businesses in our country. Women begin businesses 150% more than men, and their businesses generate more revenue.

3. Female-founded businesses generate 12% more revenue. They enjoy much, much less funding for their businesses. Women-led businesses get 1/8 the funding.

4. When men and women stack up with each other for money, there is a pay gap. Women make about 79% of what men do for the same work.

5. The average credit scores for women run 670 – for men, 675 – for women and the open credit cards run 3 for men and 3.7 for women.

6. Forty-four percent of men have paid off their student debt three years after graduation, whereas only one-third of women have paid off their debt.

7. Average rainy-day funds for men is $58,000; $33,500 for women.

8. Men have about 50% more in their retirement savings accounts than women. This is the reality of work for women. We tend to have multiple jobs – one of them termed a side hustle.

9. The number of US women with two jobs is on the rise – 7.3 million in 2015, 7.8 million in 2016. There are nearly 8 million more workers that hold two or more jobs – and the majority is women.

10. Six out of 10 US adults don't have $500 for an emergency.

With any side hustle, personal initiative is a key. And entrepreneurs – particularly the self-employed – are the drivers of their success.

We come back to confidence; the key to success. The good news is that no matter where any of us stand, with confidence, we can grow it. Everyone is attracted to confidence. Women dig it, and men love it. Confidence adds hair, drops 10 pounds, and takes off ten years.

We must be on the lookout for confidence killers like

- Perfectionism, fear of failure and over thinking things.

- Engage the confidence builders; what's already working.

- Take action. That is a big one for me – and that is what I did, starting with that hot room. I was already taking action by going back to that room at least once a day, sometimes more than once.

- Attack the "Whys."

Addressing things requires us to face them. We have to know what we are addressing. In coaching, we call the confidence killers the saboteur or the gremlin. It's what's holding you back and what might be the made-up stories of why something may not seem possible. That's one of my definitions.

Embrace crutches. Gratitude equals joy. And get a friend. So here are some things that I've learned in my journey.

- Take action.

- Stay afraid, but do it anyway.

- What's important is the action.

- You do not have to wait to be confident.

- Just do it. And eventually, the confidence will follow.

- Attack the whys. Identify them. When you think "I can't," ask "why is that?" And I invite you to continue asking why, because that saboteur is going to give you a lot of explanations to try to talk you into sticking in that place of non-action.

Embrace the confidence crutches. Using a confidence crutch is okay. Find things that give you confidence in your appearance. Use every powerful moment to the max. And answer ordinary questions in extraordinary ways. Express joy.

Embrace the Everys! "Every morning, I give thanks to God, and I spend as much time in prayer and worship and dialogue and listening – listening more than dialogue, please – for His will to be expressed for me, and for me to have been able to express enough that I have surrendered everything to Him."

But some concrete everys recommendations are:

- Making sure that I have my base, my body, in good standing.

- I'm healthy

- That I wear good undergarments – so I have a nice, complete look that is beautiful in people's eyes, looks appropriate for each situation. Having a good demeanor and a good presentation, I'm allowing people to focus on the moment of why we are there – as opposed to being distracted by something that is not appropriate. And that can be applied to jewelry, makeup, color – any of that. Those are our basic everys for the person that is out there in the world making impressions on other people.

- If social media is an area of interest, help another female entrepreneur, once a day. Tell her about your once-a-day quest.

- Confidence is a woman's most beautiful accessory — and it is her best business tool.

- When I went to work for Ruby Ribbon, my first step was to wear the product.

- I bought a product, and I went from being a woman who was continually jiggling my shoulders and adjusting my underwire bra and pulling in the back to try to — you know, you name it, I was doing it. By the time I was pulling into that parking lot, that thing was unsnapped and ready to rip off.

One of the ladies that worked for me invited me to a Ruby Ribbon party. I said, "What is that?" She said, "They will have wine." I said, "I'll be there." And I tried it. I bought one. And, the day that I wore my cami, I went from that situation of pulling it off in the parking lot too — I did not remember that I even had an undergarment until that evening when I was putting on my pajamas.

Well, I bought more, gave away my bras, and I thought that would be it. There was, though, still something tugging at me. It seems to be a unique company because I come from a background of always being in corporate America which is for me all about the money. It was a new place to be and looking at a company that's more of a sisterhood, a girlfriend-type of thing. So I think that's what continued to draw me to look at this situation that I'd never seen before — curiosity. And I realized that I could be more involved than just a client — not that there's anything wrong with that.

I decided to invest a couple of hundred dollars, which I could manage. I saw this as a ministry hobby because it was something that I believed in, that I wanted to share with other women.

My Gift below is helpful in terms of opening up and affirming the fact that your life is, in fact, full of possibilities – no matter what your level of confidence. It helps you start to attack the whys, because it asks you to address yourself and your body – to see if there are any areas that you want to change.

Download Olga's Gift HERE:
http://bit.ly/VIPWardrobe

OLGA MONROE BIOGRAPHY

Olga Monroe was born in Havana, Cuba and grew up in Raleigh, NC. She received her Bachelors' Degree in Business & Economics and Master of Arts in Liberal Science from North Carolina State University. After several decades in the Financial Industry, Olga stayed home home-school her children. As the kids got older, Olga ran several home-based businesses in a variety of industries.

One of her favorite endeavors is teaching Bikram Hot Yoga, which deepened her awareness of the human body so that after a short hiatus back in the corporate world, the discomfort of traditional underwire bras seemed excruciating. She knew there had to be another way!

That's when Olga discovered Ruby Ribbon, and liked their holistic method of support and comfort which deeply resonated with Olga. That's when she decided to step into her infinite potential!

As a Leader & Senior Stylist with Ruby Ribbon Olga is able to unite her business, leadership & personal coaching skills in a thriving atmosphere. She loves seeing others happy and thriving.

She resides in her hometown of Raleigh, NC with her two grown children, husband & rescue shelter beagle!

ASHLEY MORRISON

I AM A little younger than most business owners I know. I had one year between graduating from college and starting my company. I still refer to that year as my "lost year." It was a time that I had professors tell me that I was going to be working in sales and be in sales for the first ten years of my career, whether I liked it or not. I found out that I was very good at sales. In fact, I was spectacular at it. And, I felt like marketing and sales should not be separate.

I felt like there were so many marketing elements that could've made my efficiency better. It could've made me a more effective sales-person, and me being an entrepreneur, would walk up to bosses and tell them that. It created a lot of strife, even while most of the time I was right. That made it worse!

I discovered that I did not fit well being told to sit and cold call eight hours a day; there are so many better ways to market a business. So, during my lost year, I interviewed at a handful of small businesses and had so many say "I need help like this. And I need you, but I can't afford to hire you full-time." My hearing that resounding "I need you, but I can't have you," and asking, "Is there somebody else out there that could help you?" and hearing, "I don't know" or "I'm pretty sure no," really sparked my awakening. That was when I knew it was time for me to be a small business owner. And, it was time for me to help small business owners.

What alerted me to my awakening was seeing a consistent pattern of not fitting in and struggling in positions. I remember one event attending a very well known Christian band concert, and I heard the song "Thrive" with lyrics saying that we're meant to thrive and that we're meant for so much more than just this day-to-day activities. By now I hated getting up in the morning, hated going to work and everything about it. A sea of people surrounding me, all sitting at their desks felt the same way – and that's where that clear second vision emerged from, "I don't want employees feeling like I did, or hiding in the bathroom like I occasionally did or ever, ever having to feel like that."

Those were my two clear visions and my big push to be a small business owner came from.

I resisted being an entrepreneur all my life. In high school, I was part of DECA, an organization that puts high school students together and has them either develop and write a business plan or put on a business role-playing event, where students have to figure out what to do to solve a problem. There was something about just changed me. I competed very well with DECA.

Then I attended NC State and saw that a lot of classes I was taking in marketing were corporate level. I continued to ask questions like "What does this mean for a small business?" And the response? "Don't ask questions like that." I learned to stop asking questions. It was a pattern I kept seeing.

I tried an accounting position for a while (once my major for a couple of weeks), and then a professor advised me NOT to do that. So moving into entrepreneurship was coming for a long time. I was 'listening' for the signs, so when they showed up, I recognized them and took action.

My next step after the concert, a few months later, I opened my business. There two steps I took at the same time: one was marketing research to get a good idea as to the need in the market for marketing services and what those needs looked like. The second was asking for and getting the help I needed to develop a business plan; what my company would look like. I went to Wake Tech for that, met Katie Gailes, the director of entrepreneurship who helped walked me through that process of writing a business plan and getting everything started.

These two steps work for any business. The best businesses do their research. You can have a great idea, yet without a market for it, success is elusive. I found it heartbreaking to watch how that great idea never came to be.

Ask for help. There are so many great nationwide, international organizations that offer free resources that will help. Take advantage of every free resource out there.

I realize my jump from school to corporate to my own business was an extremely fast turnaround time. I'm one of those people that when I get an idea or an awakening or calling, it's time to do something. I don't pause. I start running toward it. What takes some a year or two with a lot of 'thinking about,' that's not me. However, let me point out this way of being doesn't always work for me. It's important to think through all the things that could happen. At the same time, it's important not to develop analysis paralysis. If you overthink and do too much work, you stew in it, never getting to the point of being in action toward what you want.

My gift below walks through how to market a business and how to think through who your target audience is. That is one of the most critical problems you'll find is, not knowing who your target audience is — and trust me, it is not everybody with a face.

On that note, avoid ever telling anybody your target market is anybody who has a face! You have to be very specific — and the more you know who they are, the better you'll be able to market to them. It'll also help develop marketing research to determine if your business is going to do well. If you're already in business, you'll see how to make your marketing campaigns work better for you – and determine what marketing campaigns you need.

My best piece of advice is "just do it" (Nike). There are so many people who are on the sidelines and scared and worried about the risk, but you've heard, and it is true that the more significant the risk, the bigger the reward. There are plenty of experts out there to help you.

Download Ashley's Gift HERE:
https://abundantmarketingsm.com/telesummit-giveaway/

ASHLEY MORRISON BIOGRAPHY

Ashley Morrison is the president and founder of Abundant Marketing. Abundant Marketing is a small business marketing company that will do anything a small business needs to grow – without breaking the bank.

Ashley is passionate about serving small business owners and helping other business owners reach their goals. As for her company, she has two clear visions for her company: (1) Create a phenomenal marketing company that helps small business grow, not only in Raleigh but around the country! and (2) Establish a workplace that employee will love to come to and love to serve our customers! Every day, she gets up and strives to reach those two goals more than she did the day before!

Ashley and her team offer free marketing strategy sessions to all small businesses simply to help small business owners brainstorm through their marketing efforts. Don't hesitate to contact the team to set up a strategy session now.

DEBORAH ORONZIO

MY AWAKENING ALL started with a voicemail. I was in my office at a local technical college, ready to counsel a community member interested in starting their own small business. There was a scheduled break in our conversation — and I was listening to my voicemail. The message was from our director of human resources, inviting me to a meeting with her and the Vice President the following Tuesday. Now, this was a Friday. You know how you have one of those, "I just know what's going to happen" moments?

While I did not appreciate the way that it was delivered (before a weekend); so be it. I knew that the college was going to tell me, "Your services are no longer needed." It was one heart-wrenching weekend. Tuesday morning I mustered up all of my fortitude and strength and went to the meeting, and yes, that's exactly what I was told!

Here's what is interesting: this was not the first time I'd heard those very words. I had been transitioned out of an existing position some five times over the course of my career; business conditions or whatever the case may be. At that moment, as I walked out of the office, I said to myself, "You know what? I have given my blood, sweat, and tears to a variety of companies and a variety of institutions over the course of my career. I've always strived to give it my best shot. And it doesn't look like I'm very much appreciated."

I am someone with an entrepreneurial spirit – although I'm not sure I recognized it at the time. Others around me would have defined it as, "She's always rocking the boat." And yes, I was always rocking the boat – to me, in the interest of positive change and progress.

I told myself, "That is it! I am no longer going to give my blood, sweat, and tears to someone else. If I'm going to do this, I'm going to step out on my own and do it." I made the decision and had no idea what I was going to do!

I had explored the concept of starting my own business earlier in my career; however, my dilemma was always, "What am I good at? And what drives me, with purpose and passion, which represents a path that I want to pursue?" The next step that I took, after leaving the college, was to start thinking about the possibility of coaching. I had explored in the past – and when I was honest with myself, I believe that it was my fear that stopped me from pursuing it several years earlier.

This time, even though I was afraid, there was simply something inside of me that said, "You have got to move forward with this." I spent the summer doing a lot of networking, looking up people whom I knew were coaches – and having interviews with them, to ask, "What was their defining moment? How did they decide that they were going to pursue this type of an opportunity in their lives?" While doing some practical research as it related to the coaching schools available, I attended a networking meeting, and there was a young, vibrant woman there who was the speaker. As it turns out she was a coach. She gave us her talk and invited us to have a free consultant with her – which I did pursue.

One fundamental question she asked me at the time was, "What's stopping you?" Because there's always something stopping us. I told her, "I'm afraid I'm too old to be doing this." She laughed, and she said to me, "Can I share something with you?" and I said, "What is that?" She said, "I came from a background of education. I was a teacher in the elementary school system. When I realized that I wanted to go out and coach people, my biggest fear was, 'I'm too young to do this. I don't have enough experience'."

That was my second defining moment, where I admitted to myself "I'll be the one standing in my own way – if I don't decide to pursue this." During that time I started to get an inkling about the idea that decision is an action in and of itself. When we were undecided about things, or when we resist walking through any fears we might have, it paralyzes us.

From that moment I started doing more and more networking. But the networking circles I was engaging with at that time had a lot to do with personal development. It was something that I was always attracted to, and I'd pursued a little bit here and a little bit there – but I had never pursued it full force. Why? Because I was trapped in the corporate world. And what do you do when you're in the corporate world? You give the companies you work for 50 to 60 or plus hours of your working week – and if you have a family, in many cases, that's what takes up the rest.

At this point, I now had some free time to pursue this. I liked what I was experiencing. I realized up until that time I hadn't been standing up for myself or investing in myself enough to explore. I hadn't thought about what it is I love to do and what I'm good at doing.

I continued to be drawn to this idea of, "I'd love to be able to coach people and mentor them in some way." I started reaching out to people who were doing just that – so that I could learn, "Well, what was it like for them? How did they go about the process of, let's say, remaking themselves or reinventing themselves?"

At the college, I taught one of the cardinal rules of stepping out of your own way is to "Learn on someone else's dime." In other words, take the opportunity to reach out to people who have been there, done that – and hopefully, they will be gracious enough, which most of them were, to help you – to help to guide you – and to share with you mistakes that they may have made. And they may be able to help you circumvent those same mistakes.

I was introduced to that concept of creating a vision for myself first through the mentoring program and secondarily, through another program that I had learned about – which is called the DreamBuilder Program, developed by Mary Morrissey, a world-renowned personal development expert. The simplest way that I like to describe Dream-Building is that we start with teaching ourselves how to conduct what I call transformational thinking.

Sounds like a big, hoity-toity term, right? All that it means is that we learn the techniques to think beyond our current circumstance so that we can imagine what is possible in our lives. By stimulating the imagination, we can then move forward to create a vision in our mind. We actually map out our lives in our mind. I learned the vision we create in our mind is as real as anything that's happening around us. It simply has not manifested in physical realities yet.

One of the things that we've discussed in your program and Mary's program as well is this concept that thoughts become things.

To imagine and to record – meaning writing it down or recording it in some way – what is possible and what it is that we know deep down inside we are longing to do, it gives us hope. And in having hope, it builds our confidence.

One thing I would like to stress is that the action doesn't have to be big. It can be teeny, tiny, baby steps. But it's teeny, tiny, baby steps in the direction of our dreams – and when we can continually do that, holding that vision of who we want to be and where we want to be – consistently in our mind – it's amazing what comes forth.

In my workshops, I asked attendees to "Write out your vision for yourself as best you can." And of course, it's usually their very first stab at ever taking the opportunity to do something like this. The guide-lines I use are 1. Start with the phrase "I am so happy and grateful now that...." and we write out our vision as vividly as possible, almost as though we were handwriting what a videographer would capture on a camera. With the key being – everything is written in the present tense – as though it has already happened. So what does that say? That it's not a place we are striving to go. It is a place and a mindset where we start living that way from that moment forward.

As a career strategist and coach, I'd like to work with people focusing on the vision that they want to create for their career path.

My gift below includes ten questions to ask yourself "If anything were possible, what would you love to be doing?"

Download Deborah's Gift HERE:
https://selfempowercoaching.com/landing-page-create-career-vision

DEBORAH ORONZIO BIOGRAPHY

Deborah Oronzio is the founder of Self-Empower Coaching whose mission is to help motivated professionals achieve not only success but also experience satisfaction and significance in their careers. She helps people explore the next phases of their career path whether that is advancement within their established career or carving out a completely new path including the start-up of their own business. She holds two certifications in coaching, one from The Life Mastery Institute as a DreamBuilder Coach and the second from The Coach Training Alliance.

Deb has a deep and diverse background in business, training and education. She spent considerable time in the medical diagnostics industry primarily in the areas of marketing and management. Her most recent positions were Director of Entrepreneurship and Business/Marketing Instructor at Wake Tech Community College. She is an active SCORE business mentor, and also volunteers as a career coach for Dress for Success. She not only works with aspiring and existing entrepreneurs but also with those who are seeking new career opportunities. Her primary interest is in helping folks to explore and cultivate their mindset concerning their entrepreneurial or job-seeking experiences. She is adept in facilitating the process of designing and developing the vision for their business or career. She frequently counsels in the areas of business planning and effective marketing techniques including branding.

DIVYA PAREKH

I WANT TO start the story of my awakening by sharing what it means to "knight yourself." I have to go back to my childhood to explain. It's a story from a play I was doing at an all-girls middle school where girls participated and role-played as men. I was a soldier, and then came the queen. The queen took her sword, put it on my head, and said, "By the power vested in me, I knight you, Thee." Because of the queen, I got the position of authority and leadership for a long time. After the play, when I was talking with my dad, I asked him, "Why does the queen have the power to knight me?" My dad said, "You have the power to knight yourself, Divya. You don't have to wait for the queen."

That story and my dad's message stuck with me for the rest of my life. So, "knight yourself" means taking ownership of the message that you're living, of the story you're sharing with others, and knighting yourself.

My life journey involved adventure and enchantment. In 2008, the economy took a tumble, and layoffs were common. It impacted all industries. Coming from a science background, I saw that even the biopharmaceutical industry was affected. One day, the rumor of layoffs came true. Several of my colleagues, my friends, walked out with years of work and memories in one cardboard box. It was a life-changing moment. It felt like there was a sword hanging over my head. It could drop, and the possibility of losing my job was genuine.

Although I had my job, something deep stirred within me. In that moment of realization, I decided to take charge of my career. I could design my destiny. As I reflected, my insatiable thirst for learning and passion for making an impact led me to coaching. As a coach, I had the privilege to partner with people, supporting them to experience "a-ha" life moments, to step into their genius—and have that awakening we're talking about. It was so rewarding; I stepped into it.

A few years later, I was invited to participate in an anthology. My first thought was that writing a chapter for the book would be easy, as I had years of technical writing experience. Usually, my professional writing was received well. I felt like a poet taking her first step into the book wonderland. It was an excellent way to start. I was confident in my skills to complete my contribution.

I began my writing journey thinking that three months was plenty of time to write. It was going to be a piece of cake. There were no experiments to be described, no data to be analyzed, no anomalies to be explained, and no conclusions to be drawn. There was a whole lot more that goes into writing scientific papers that I wouldn't have to worry about with this chapter. I typed, I wrote, I journaled. I used my phone to record and got it transcribed. I would write, read the printed word, ball it up, and throw it away. The ideas were not gelling. I tried everything I could think of to get this chapter written. Every attempt ended either in the online or offline trash. I guess that the reason for the difficulty I was experiencing was the fact that I was writing about my "why" and my vision, which was a very different kind of writing for me.

At three months, my publisher reached out to me for my chapter. I asked for an extension and then another one. I extended the three-month deadline to six months. She was very patient, but it finally wore thin. She suggested that I be involved in the next anthology instead of this one. She shared that the delay was impacting the other authors. The realization that I, who prided myself on being a coach, was a roadblock hit me hard. The awareness brought the recognition that I feared success. Once I faced my fears, the jolt spurred me to action. I requested the last extension.

So, being a scientist, I hypothesized my experiment. I already had my topic and background information. All I had to do was research. I went and purchased many programs from world-class leaders that shared how to write a book. Because I resorted to finding help, I was finally able to churn out a pretty good chapter. Learning from these masters was eye-opening for me. I kept on learning; it's my nature, and the key is to keep on mastering your craft. I faced a few challenges when I wrote my next book, but it was much more comfortable than the first one.

One of my first coaching instructors had shared that it is essential to have a coach in your corner. High performers, regardless of their industry, usually have a success coach. It's like driving a car. No matter how long we drive, we all have blind spots. It is crucial to know the blind spots and how to overcome them.

Then, I finished writing my third book. The process seemed simple and fast. During our VIP Intensive Day, I updated my coach on my progress. He pondered and said, "I think you've got something here with your writing." I asked him what he meant. He countered my question with this question: "How did you write your third book?"

I was explaining how I wrote my book. As a good coach does, he asked me, "How did you write your second book? And how are you planning to write your fourth book?" As I was telling him, he said, "Divya, you already have a process. You're following it. So, why don't you narrow it down? And why don't you document the process, cement it? Make it concrete. And see how it plays out." I started using that process, and I have now written 12 books! It works every time. My coach raised my awareness of my strengths. This growth consciousness further led to the privilege and honor of helping scores of people take their books from ideas to becoming the springboards for their businesses by using this same process.

Initially, the aspiring authors would say, "Divya, I don't know how to write. Divya, I don't have enough time to write. I don't know where to begin. I'm not an author. I am not a good enough writer. I am not qualified to write a book. I need a publisher or a book deal. I need a ton of content to write. I don't know what the book will do for me." As our partnerships blossomed, I had the fortune to see their depth of self-discovery. Gradually, the writing journey became a beautiful awakening process. Authors perceived stepping out of their comfort zones as the opportunity for personal and professional growth. For me, it's not just about writing a book; it's about learning and personal growth. It's about growing into your dreams.

One of my authors described the writing process as forming a pearl. A grain of sand causes irritation to the oyster. The oyster has two options. It could either let the grain cause irritation, or the oyster could deal with the grain of sand, morphing the pain into a pearl. There's a difference between writing a blog, an article, or even a Facebook post and writing a book. Similarly, an aspiring author or an author could either run away from writing or lean into the discomfort. Those who lean in gain clarity, learn, develop, and evolve into a pearl. There's just something magical about writing a book. In my experience, it's not unlike birthing a child. You are sharing your pearl with others. I can share this because I have personally experienced it myself as well as had the joy of experiencing it with amazing authors!

My hope for you is that you experience the joy and fulfillment our family of authors has experienced. If you want to and are ready to begin writing your book, you may use my gift below, which is a five-day writing challenge. The key is committing. Say to yourself, "You know what? I'm starting this, and I'm going to complete the exercise every single day." Your commitment will lead to momentum.

You will start out by determining your preferred mode of writing and continue gaining further insights into book writing. By the end of the fifth day, you will finish the first paragraph of your book!

Remember what my dad said: "Don't wait for somebody. Go knight yourself." After you write your first paragraph, I would love to hear your success story at contact@divyaparekh.com. Then, with your permission, I would like to share your success story with thousands of my followers to inspire them to form their very own pearls.

Download Divya's gift HERE:
https://success.divyaparekh.com/5daywritingchallenge

DIVYA PAREKH BIOGRAPHY

Divya Parekh is a 4-time #1 International best-selling author, keynote speaker, business relationship and book writing coach who has had great success with entrepreneurs, coaches, aspiring authors, and speakers. Divya's books and strategies have been endorsed by the likes of Brian Tracy, Marshall Goldsmith, Kevin Harrington (Shark Tank), James Malinchak (ABC's Secret Millionaire), Sherry Winn (Two-time Olympian) and many more....

Whether Divya is speaking, advising corporate clients, coaching business owners or helping authors to write their books and get published, she has a message that is essential to bringing success to anyone.

That message has five tenets:

1. Servant Leadership

2. Collaboration, not Competition

3. Build Relationships that matter

4. Mindfulness works everywhere

5. Knight yourself.

JUDY PROKOPIAK

I HAD TO think about my awakening moment. I want to go back to 2008, I had some gynecologic outpatient surgery, and that was going to be just fine. Everything was going to be okay. Shortly after that, I went into a full-blown autoimmune response, autoimmune – we didn't even know what was going on. I was just sick: bleeding, belly and gut problems, and allergies and all kinds – just one thing after another.

Six months of this struggle – on top of the fact that I had 35 years of shame, unworthiness, depression, chronic fatigue, and an eating disorder. I already had a lot of baggage, and now all of this was piled on top of it. And then I began struggling and suffering and could barely get out of bed. Working as a swim coach at the time, all I could do was go to the pool in the morning, then come home and lay in the bed; then go back to the pool the next day.

As I lay in bed, with my husband lovingly taking care of me, I told him, "I think you need to put me in a nursing home because I don't think I can keep living like this." I said it jokingly, but honestly, I was feeling like, "I can't imagine living the rest of my life like this!"

Being a nurse, I tried to be my own advocate. The truth is, when you are sick and tired, exhausted and overwhelmed, and depressed and in pain, it's tough to be your own advocate. It seemed hard for me to step out and ask for things I wanted. My husband kissed me and said, "You'll figure it out. It'll all be okay."

Sharing this is giving me chills right now. That was the wake-up moment for me, and I said to myself, "Take back control over your health and your life" and "You can figure this out." "You're a nurse. You're a diabetic" "What? Of course, I can figure this out." Right?

That was the moment that I went, "Okay." Then came, of course, "Now what am I going to do? I thought I was already doing every-thing," listening to the doctors and following their plans."

A big step for me was that I started getting busy watching online summits! This was ten years ago, and they were brand new. I don't think they were even called that then. I remember hearing some-body talking about gluten and leaky gut and autoimmune conditions. I thought "Okay, I don't know, but that sounds like what I have! It sounds like what's going on with me."

Next step: I went 'all in' and got books and learned. Then at some point, I tapped into my inner wisdom, my intuition which is what we are talking about.

I was waking up to my potential. We know the power we have, and we have all the answers, yet we're always looking out there some-where for our answers.

So I tapped into my being a nurse, and yet I would go to the doctor and tell him I thought I had a gluten problem, or a lactose problem, or some kind of colitis. And I was sure I was allergic to things. And every time the doctor would say that I was right. I didn't want to be right! I wanted to be well.

As a nurse with twenty years of knowledge and experience, I was a diabetes educator and a swim coach, so I knew about nutrition and sports and the body and how it worked — and here I was, struggling myself. I was 'in' my own story, so I couldn't see what I could see when helping others. I had to step out of myself.

Because I knew what I was talking about I started to have all this compassion for all of the patients that I had served over the years and realized they too are struggling. I continued on my journey, learning, healing, food, nutrition, trying different things and trying to figure it all out. Had I known there was a thing called a health coach or a mentor I may have gotten well sooner. It took me a lot of years to figure it out with lots of trial and error.

My final diagnosis was autoimmune colitis. My mom died of autoimmune pulmonary fibrosis. I was already developing scarring in my lungs, same kind of thing. This was what was causing all the other problems.

So fast forward. My health is better, and I decide to become a health coach. It was the perfect way to help people. I found that their stories, their shame, and their unworthiness and baggage were exactly what I saw in myself.

I wanted and needed to heal these stories and got another wake-up call in 2015. I was attending a health coaching workshop. My mom, gone ten years, came to me and I heard her say, "Wake up. Wake up, Judy. Wake up. It's time to wake up. Make your mess your message." I started crying, and I was thinking, "What mess? What message? There are so many." That was when I started healing. And I realized that my problem was a thinking problem. I need a new way to think. I need to get some help from a coach or mentor.

Because I'm a swimmer, I ran to the pool at the hotel and started swimming and crying in the water. I let my tears flow. Somehow later I found myself journaling, pouring it all out. All the memories seemed to want to be released.

Next, I began to think about what am I going to do with all of this. I'm in tears day after day, crying and blubbering, yet it was beautiful and healing.

It felt like I had never really felt my feelings. I had always squashed them, ate them, pushed them down and down.

I saw my mom depressed and I told myself I would just suck it up and 'swim' through life. And I saw that I did not know how to manage my mind or my feelings.

I started looking online, summits again and found a hypnotherapist to help me. Then I discovered Mary Morrissey and her DreamBuilder program and wondered if I needed a dream. I didn't know, and I hadn't dreamed in some 30 years. Then I heard Mary say that our thoughts create our feelings, then our actions, which create our results. Wow. Why didn't they teach this in fourth grade? Why didn't I know this?

So first steps were simply to start writing, like a brain dump or download. Get it out of your head because if you are like me, it kept going around and around and around and I was stuck and could not get out of my own way until I started writing.

As you write you begin to get clarity; things like "I'm still angry at my dad" or "I'm really shaming myself." Getting it out on paper allowed me to get the emotion out. Then I was able to start separating words from emotions. Then I was clear enough to ask what I needed next; what kind of help do I need.

You could start with a friend and share what happened, what came out. I didn't need fixing; I needed to share, was all.

I love videos, so I made a video as my Gift for you below. It's about 20 minutes, and it's called "Your Journey Back to Health Starts with A Dream." We all need a vision and to answer questions like why we want to be healthy or what will you do with your life.

When you answer those questions, you will be inspired to take action on your health. I didn't want to be sick anymore. I had to grind it out for myself. Perhaps you will not have to.

You cannot access your potential when both your health and mind are suffering. You are not able to fully bring your gifts to the world. I thought of myself as a good woman doing good work in the world – I was doing a lot. Yet I was a human doing, not a human being.

Download Judy's Gift HERE:
https://www.judyprokopiak.com/your-journey-back-to-health-starts-with-a-dream

JUDY PROKOPIAK BIOGRAPHY

Judy Prokopiak or Coach Judy as her friends and fans call her, has been coaching in some form for over 15 years. As the head coach of a competitive swim team she parlayed that experience into health, life and mindset coaching when she had to go on her own journey to better health.

As a nurse and diabetes educator for over 22 years, Judy was determined to find answers and she did. She found not only food and nutrition to support her well being, she also discovered that much of her suffering was because of the her own thinking. Beliefs and Stories of shame, unworthiness, perfectionism kept her stuck in grief, depression and anxiety.

She discovered that she needed a new way to think a new way to be and to learn to take back control over her thoughts. It's always a thinking problem. She now helps women in some kind of life transition to wake up, stop sleepwalking through life and dare to dream another dream.

MARIE SNIDER

WHEN I FIRST started in the business world after teaching for several decades, I worked for my daughter for three-and-a-half years in her marketing business. When she closed that business – I was adrift. I started to think about what I was really good at. I already knew I was good at helping others find their voice. I can teach an elevator speech to a dog – and it will be successful!

I was also really very good at the 10-minute speech; the kind people do in networking groups. I knew I could help so many people. Of course, my passion, having taught for over 30 years, is to educate and to help people. I see myself as a person who really makes a difference in other people's lives, particularly those in business. That's very exciting to me. I love helping them.

My awakening moment arrived was when I was 13 years old, sitting at the dinner table with my family. We always had Sunday dinner together. We discussed current events, and it was typically a two-hour event. During dessert that night, my brothers started to talk about college. My oldest brother was going to college the next year, and then the brother in between was going two years after that; I was going after his first year. So there would be three of us in college at the same time.

My mother looked up and smiled and said, "Well, you know, Marie, it's not as important for women to go to college. After all, the boys will be the breadwinners." I felt like I was having a heart attack. I couldn't breathe. I just sat there, absolutely stunned, and I said to myself, "Oh, my God. They can't pay for me to go to college. What am I going to do?"

My first step came about two minutes later when I said to myself, "Okay after dinner's over, I'm going to make a plan." And I did. I said, "First I am going to get on the Honors list at school. Then I'm going to try to see if I can join organizations in school." I joined the French Club and the track team. When I was young, there were no scholarships for women for track or being in the French Club. So I looked around, and one of my friends took me to a festival of one-act plays. The award for the best actress – who happened to be from my school – was half a year's tuition at a women's college! I thought, "I can do that" even though I had never been in a play before.

I started auditioning for everything. I was in action. If it was within two busses and a train from where I lived, I took two buses and a train – and I was acting and singing. I started taking voice lessons. I was dedicated to my mission. I won many trophies on the way to that vital competition – and by my senior year, I was ready to win! We were doing The Miracle Worker. So I had to be Helen Keller. I went around the house for three weeks with earmuffs and a blindfold on, trying to figure out how being blind would feel. By the time the auditions came around, I got the part. And when we did the show, I won the prize! My awakening and my first few action steps allowed me to have the financing for half of my year at school. And the other thing that I was doing at the same time was ramping up my academics to get on the Honors list.

At my high school, there was even a test to get into the high school. I was in the top 25; they didn't ask you what you were going to take. They told you what you would take. They did the choosing. I had never made the Honor Roll, posted every quarter in the main hall, including all the names and their GPAs – down to the third decimal point. I started working harder and harder at academics – so much so that, when I was the lead in the senior play, people were running all around and singing and laughing – and I was doing my homework. Because I had to do my homework.

On the last day of school, when I went to clean out my locker, I check the Honors post to see how I had done – to see if I'd made the top 25. And I was number 1! I was overwhelmed, touched, and could hardly believe it. I knew I'd worked hard enough to make it happen, but the rest of those girls were really smart, too.

I had another awakening when working with my daughter at her marketing firm. One of my jobs was to do business networking. I saw how the elevator speech worked; how some were very successful with it, and some people were not. It was about that time my daughter closed her marketing firm, and it occurred to me that I could help the people who were not doing effective networking. I could teach them how to do elevator speeches. I could teach them how to do 10-minute speeches. I can make a difference for these people. They're selling good products and services, and I wanted to help them.

The idea to do this came when I was sitting in a local leads group. There was a gentleman who had just moved to North Carolina from Kentucky. Anyone could tell that he'd never been asked to do this kind of elevator speech. He had a computer with him, and people had said that he had worked on their computers. He got up for his elevator speech, and he mumbled so no one could hear or understand him. You could tell it was hard for him and he was embarrassed and afraid. Although he offered an excellent service, I could see people discounting him – and perhaps thinking he wasn't competent because of how he presented himself. I felt terrible for him.

I chatted with him during the break and asked him if I could help him with his elevator speech. I gave him a few tips – but he was not open to much more than that. While I never saw him again, I realized I could make a big difference helping people with what was easy for me, and hard for them to do.

I always help my clients understand that when they speak, they are serving others and it's not really about them. It's still about the client and the help they need.

I love helping people find a way that they can share their expertise with others people will take them up on that offer.

I think people fear public speaking because they feel exposed; like you're naked. That's why people came up with the idea of picturing the audience naked. While I don't recommend that, it is important to remember that you have something of value to give them. When you speak to them, you are making them aware of this wonderful product. My work is more of a kindness rather than a sales business.

In my gift below, you will find some simple bullet points and suggestions for your elevator speech and a 10-minute presentation.

Download Marie's Gift HERE:
http://eepurl.com/dtJITr

MARIE SNIDER BIOGRAPHY

Marie Snider was born in Ohio and attended private Catholic schools from kindergarten through college. At Ursuline College, she completed a double major in English and Theatre and a minor in Secondary Education. (That created a massive load of credit hours per semester!!) She earned her M.A. in theatre at Case Western Reserve University. She is fond of saying that "a master's degree in theatre and $3.50 will get you a regular cup of coffee almost anywhere." Following grad school, Marie performed with a professional improvisation company called The End Result Cult for about two years.

Marie taught English, speech, and theatre in private schools in Ohio for ten years then moved to North Carolina to enjoy the Carolina blue sky and Southern charm. She started her company in 2013 and is one of the contributing authors of the Amazon best selling business book, 17 Legal Ways to Double Your Income.

In October of 2016, Marie was a key speaker at the Excelerate Experience, a one day business conference at the NC BioTech Center in Research Triangle Park, North Carolina. In March of 2017, she spoke at the Carolina Business Woman's Conference.

After retiring from the world of public school, Marie became the Production Manager and Executive Assistant at SA Brown Marketing Strategy. She enjoyed the fast-paced world of tradeshow and event planning and is a member of Meeting Planners International. For fun, Marie sings. She is a member of the Durham Savoyards, sings in her church choir, and in the shower.

LYNDAH TELLO

My awakening came when I became a new entrepreneur. I knew I needed to get out into the world and meet people who were going to be potential customers or referral partners. Like many I suspect, I did that to make those valuable acquaintances and connections. I was, however, having challenges with networking groups that were 'seat specific.' I would find that my seat was already taken. And I can honestly say I experienced some negativity and just not fitting in with the girls. They didn't vote me in, and they didn't allow me to join the group. I always say they voted me off the island to kind of make light of it. It was so like being the It Girl table in high school, but it is now thirty years later!

I remember thinking to myself, "You know what? I can't be alone in this experience. There have to be other girls that have been left out." I don't know if it was because I was overweight or didn't wear enough makeup. I didn't know what the problem was, only that the real problem was theirs: they were unable to perceive my worth and the value I bring. That's when I took those lemons and made lemonade.

I had another realizing as well. If I paid $500 to join a group, the person sitting across from you might not be somebody I hold in high regard. I don't know that I would want to give referrals to somebody just because they invested $500 to join. I wanted to refer people because I thought well of them – because my referrals are my valuables. I'm saying to the person, "I endorse who I'm sending you to." Not just because they happened to have invested to sit across the table from me.

Then I noticed that when I went to these groups, I felt like I had invisible dollar signs above my head. People would count on me to buy their product or service. I knew why. They wanted to recoup their investment. They wanted their money back in a sale from me. They didn't want to know me. They didn't care about my business. "This is yucky," I remember thinking. I had the $500> I didn't see it as a good investment. I didn't want to be in a group where new people arrived and were pounced on. I didn't want to be obligated to refer to somebody who I didn't think well of. I wanted to have genuine referrals – the way they're supposed to be. And I wanted to focus on the relationship and have real referral partners. I realized very quickly; I didn't want to be short-sighted and have someone as a customer. I wanted to refer to you and have you reciprocate. I wanted to help you grow your business, and you help me grow my business. That was worth way more because I could give you ten leads, and you could give me ten leads. That's much more valuable than one customer.

So I saw that these groups were missing something very valuable. They were not focusing on relationships. They were also expensive, which kind of made people fall into that trap of wanting to recoup that investment. I met a few people who joined and never got any leads at all.

Seeing there were key failing points to those groups, I wanted to create an opportunity that eliminated those pain points, that would be successful. I felt happy that I started out with just 20 women around a table, one chapter that met twice a month. Now I have four chapters. Meetup, the company that hosts me, flew me up to New York because of the fast growth of my group. While I was in New York and gave my speech, I got a standing ovation. The owner of Meetup came up and shook my hand and told me that I was a true visionary. The women attendees said so many times, "Hey, I want to start up a chapter. I do understand what you're trying to say. I want relationships, not just a quick sale." They got my message. They understood where I was coming from.

My final experience of joining an existing group, before I got my big awakening, they did not have a financial person at the table. Good, I thought, I can get into this group! But then they said, "Well, we want to wait 6 or 8 weeks until we have a Visitors' Day, to see if anybody else applies." So the Visitors' Day came. One other person was there, and they applied. And without even discussion, they selected the new person.

They just didn't want me. It felt like they were waiting for anyone else to come along. That's when I decided that I wasn't going to do this anymore. I realized that at some point, it felt almost like an abusive thing. "I'm not going to keep being a doormat. I'm not going to subject myself to this rejection anymore. I'm done."

I was sitting across the table after hearing this news, and I said out loud, "Boy, I'm so disappointed. I thought that I was going to be invited to join this group." And the other person across from me said, "Yeah, they rejected my application, too. And there's nobody here doing what I'm doing." Then she said, "You know, I guess they just don't like me." I told her she was in good company!

That's when I had my epiphany: I am not alone. There are lots of hard-working, intelligent, passionate women. And you know what? Maybe we're a little intimidating. I came to understand the power that I was creating. And I thought to myself, "There are other intelligent women out there that are intimidating to these small-minded ladies. And God bless them, that's fine if they want to sit and have coffee every week with each other and think how smart they are. That's not my concern. I go to work to make money. I want to make valuable connections. I want to grow my business. That's why I'm in business.

My next step, very simple: I sat down, and I made a list of things I did not like about their groups, things that I thought were not good for business. Because this is a business investment and a good investment is where everyone benefits.

Then I made a list of things that weren't appropriate business investments in my view. First and number one: mandatory attendance. If someone has a chance to make money, and they come to my meeting, I tell them not ever to turn down a chance to make money to go to the meeting. A client always trumps a meeting. Some groups have a limit as to how many absences you can have in a year, and you have to have a person to take your place. It could become like a second job to maintain it. I didn't want to be a burden to somebody. I wanted to be a blessing.

Next, I took this list of things that I thought were very valuable – and I when I was attending networking meetings, I would talk to the ladies and tell them about my vision for this new kind of group. It was to be called 1099 Ladies, so it's recognizable that it's for self-employed businesswomen. I went down my list with them and asked if they thought they would want to join. The answers were a resounding Yes! I got their contact information so when I was ready to pull the trigger; I would already have a list of interested women.

I wanted to focus on a core group of people who had experiences like mind and valued what I was doing. I wanted to create a place where I was celebrated, not tolerated. I wanted a sisterhood of women who were like-minded. I wanted to be very positive and wasn't dealing with offensive behavior.

My visit to New York and Meetup executives I told them everything was free in this group. I figured they were probably thinking, 'How does this girl make any money? Why would she do this? This is not the Salvation Army. This is a business networking group.' I told them that I believe the value of a relationship is priceless. Some people are so poor all they have is money. They didn't understand the importance of the relationship. I realized I could pay fees for this Meetup for the rest of my life and not even touch a break-even point because I have developed hundreds of relationships.

My life improved exponentially founding and launching this group. Before long someone approached me about opening another chapter.

I am growing this thing – and the owner of Meetup said, "I see this as a nationwide thing, Lyndah." Yes, I thought. Yes, it is.

I learned a valuable lesson for myself to stop existing where I am tolerated and go where I am celebrated. Go where people embrace you and welcome you. We genuinely have a deep and wonderful relationship. They could call me at 2:00 in the morning with a flat tire and I'd jump in my car to help them.

My gift below will help you solidify your vision for your business and a plan to accomplish it.

Download Lyndah's Gift HERE:
http://1099ladiesnetworking.com/wp-content/uploads/2018/05/1099-download.pdf

LYNDAH TELLO BIOGRAPHY

Born in New York City, some of Lyndah Tello's earliest forms of employment were on Wall Street. There was a *beat* there, people walked to it, talked to it, and it was both exhilarating and intoxicating! With the birth of her first child, Lyndah left that industry to begin a new career in education, allowing her to spend more time with her baby. She received her BS in education at Queens College, and MS in Environmental Science with a minor in Physics from Brooklyn College. Lyndah was a teacher in NYC and NC for over a decade. When her youngest child became independent Lyndah **realized** she was now *free* to do anything, so she returned to the financial industry.

When Lyndah went looking for a networking group so she could grow her financial business, she found that every group had strict guidelines of only one person per business category, or there was a huge cost to join.

Lyndah, being Lyndah, knew that other women needed a networking group to start their businesses but didn't have the funds to join a group or had a business like theirs that was in a group that they wanted to join. She choose to start her own; and thus, 1099 Ladies was born.

KRYSTI TURZNIK

My awakening was really so very magical. As a child and most of my life, I didn't believe in myself. I didn't believe that I had anything of value or worth to offer. So I settled into a life where I played the part of what everyone thought that I should be doing, letting my dreams and my goals become secondary. I took that message to heart. Lo and behold when I was 17, I developed a heart condition and I again settled again into a life that I knew was not the one I was supposed to be leading.

I remember specifically one day when I was in the shower, and I felt the full extent of the loss and the sadness, wondering how my life became like this and that it was completely unrecognizable. I knew I had to do something entirely different and so in the moment, I claimed it! I screamed "No" in my head and would not tolerate that — and instantly, that physical symptom disappeared. That's when I started to explore the mind-body connection. As I healed, so did my heart condition, teaching me about the power we have within. My first big awakening.

Before too long, again, I allowed myself to settle back into where I thought that I was supposed to be.

I ended up in a job that was unfulfilling, both emotionally and spiritually. That's when I had another beautiful awakening.

On one particular day I remember have a conversation with my-self about this, wondering what can I do? I needed something that would fill my soul and make me happy.

Instantly, "hypnosis" popped into my head. I found that inter-esting and followed that nudge; that inner guidance. Next, I started looking into this because while I wasn't sure where the thought came from, I knew there was something to it.

Exactly two weeks later I enrolled in my first hypnosis training. That motivated me to start doing the work that I have been doing for these past 18 years – and putting all of the pieces of my life together.

I was super motivated about this because I knew that this guid-ance was something that I wouldn't normally think of. It made me stop and pay attention to it. Had I not honored that guidance, I would have missed that awakening entirely. I permitted myself to figure out what was going on. I discovered as I was doing that, things started to flow magically. I still had to enroll in that class and show up and do the work and put myself on the path of continuing. The motivation was knowing this was where I was supposed to be.

This research and process was personal and intimate as I was aware that those around me had no idea what I was talking about.

When I did share, they thought that it was so foreign, wondered why I was doing this. It did not determine because I knew that it came from that more significant and that deeper place within, that truly was demanding to be honored. So for me, it was a solo journey.

More magic started to show up when I began to write a book, working with a book coach toward the end of the year of training. I was given a challenge of identifying some bigger influencers I would like to have endorse my book. So I put my big wish list together with my dream endorsers, and I started researching again, looking for those who had impacted my life in a big way.

I sent an email to each of them – and I shared how they changed my life, and how I would be grateful for their support and endorse-ment. And lo and behold, shortly after I did that, I got a wonderful response from one of the two people on Bernard Michael Beckwith's team, saying, "We're interested in this. Please send us a copy of the book so that they can review it." Two days later, after they had reviewed it, I was gifted with this beautiful endorsement that speaks tremendous volumes on what's contained within the book.

Before I sent each email, I centered myself. I went to that deepest place with the intention of a being clear about the purpose of this book, why I wrote it and why I wanted it out there. I visualized that when the book was received, they could honor my message and get back to me in a positive way. The majority of the people ended up responding to me, some of them gifted me their endorsements, which was beautiful.

I'll ask a question and pay attention to the first thing that pops into my mind from my intuition. It sometimes takes a while, and then out of the clear blue and all of a sudden, I'll get something I didn't expect. Sometimes I get shivers or goosebumps when I get that recognition. So it comes in many different ways.

Below you may have my Gift which is a Belief Change Workshop to help you go through the process I did. You'll write down what you are thinking and where you believe it came from.

I like to remind my clients that we are here on purpose for a purpose and that we matter. As soon as you allow yourself to step into honoring those little nudges —that you're going to be getting every single moment it's easier to walk into your infinite possibility. Permit yourself to do that.

Download Krysti's Gift HERE:
https://powerful-mind.com/beliefchange

KRYSTI TURZNIK BIOGRAPHY

Krysti Turznik is a motivational speaker who shows people how to shine light on their shadows, understand that mindset is everything, and to show up as a powerful creator in their lives so they can create a life they don't need to escape from where every day can feel like a day at the beach.

She inspires and equips people with practical tools and the desire to etch away rough edges and implement personal changes required to live a happier, healthier, and more fulfilling life.

Krysti's #1 best-selling book, Mindset Magic: Using Scientific & Spiritual Principles to Create Your Life, has been endorsed by Michael Bernard Beckwith. She holds a Master Degree in Metaphysics, Bachelor of Science Degrees in Biology and Metaphysics, is an ordained minister, and a consulting hypnotist who has been helping people improve their lives for nearly two decades.

Krysti lives in Wisconsin with her husband, daughter, and four cats.

SUSAN WALSH

I LOOK AT my awakening in an unusual way, from 'the dark night of the soul.' People usually come at infinite potential from a different place. The dark night of the soul, however, is actually the dawning of our infinite potential. Dark nights of the soul look different for everybody. It is something that challenges us at a core level – and the challenge is deep-seated, and it's tenacious. I don't think that there are any two alike, and I recommend not comparing yours to another's. There will be common ingredients, of course, and if we allow them, they'll break us open to the greatest selves we ever could have ever imagined: a version of ourselves that we never even thought possible. Not only did my dark night of the soul propel me in significant ways along my transformational path, I learned that out of our darkest nights can come our brightest hours – and that they carry within them the seeds of infinite potential.

My awakening came when I was working as an executive in banking. I became pregnant with my first child. At that time, working from home or part-time just wasn't an option. So I decided to leave my position and stay home and become a full-time mom. It was a magical time for me as I waited a long time to have a child, and I was so overjoyed to be Ryan's mommy. I would take him with me almost everywhere I went – and he was such a relaxed and happy baby. One day, when Ryan was about three months old, I was with a group of people, and I overheard two men talking. They had both lost their sons. Their sons had died, and I looked at my precious little boy, and I thought, "I could never live through that."

I was going to a wedding out of town, and I was staying with my mother who lived in Texas – and I was happy about that. As my dad had passed away several months before, I hadn't seen her since shortly after the funeral – so it was great that this happy occasion was coming up. I had completely put out of my mind that conversation those men were having. We were all really happy about this wonderful upcoming occasion.

Arriving at my mother's house, I found out that she hadn't ordered the full-size rental crib from the company I'd asked her to call. Instead, she borrowed a Port-A-Crib from a neighbor. This is a soft structure, like a playpen; not a hard wooden structure like a crib. When I first saw it, instantly I felt this sinking sensation in my gut. I wanted my baby to sleep in a real crib. By now, however, the rental place was closed, and my mother assured me that the neighbor used it for her grandchild and it was going to be perfectly fine. And so, with no other options, I agreed – knowing I was going to take care of that first thing the next morning. Next morning was the day of the wedding. Ryan wasn't awake yet, which was typical for him. He was an excellent sleeper – and I'd usually have to wake him up. When I went to wake him up, I immediately noticed that something was very, very wrong. He was in an unnatural position, and I became terrified. I rushed to the Port-A-Crib to get him out, only to discover that he was stiff and blue. A neo-natal nurse happened to live across the street, and she came over and performed CPR while I was waiting outside for the ambulance to arrive. I felt as if I was losing my mind. This can't be happening. My skin felt as if it was on fire – like somebody peeled off the outer layer, and all the nerve endings were exposed and burning.

I want you to know that you may feel like you're losing your mind; your reality is slipping away when your dark night of the soul starts. Because it is – the reality of the life you've known, it's over – and it's sometimes leaving in a cataclysmic, "Whoosh." After several hours of valiant effort by the hospital staff, they came to tell me that Ryan couldn't be saved. Just like that, I realized that life as I knew it was over. I was devastated. I managed to get to the airport, and on the flight home, I remembered thinking, "I don't want anybody else to get hurt. But if this plane were to go down, it would be okay with me."

At Ryan's wake, the first gift from the dark night of the soul came to me. People were coming up to me and giving me hugs. For the first time in my life, I could actually feel the energy – the vibrations coming from their bodies into mine. It was more like it was radiating from their body into my body – from every single person. It was such a surreal experience. I realized later that the only reason it was possible was that my ego had collapsed. It had been completely shattered by the death of my son. Normally, I wouldn't be able to experience anything like the sensation of physically feeling love from people, radiating into my body – except for the fact that the ego, which happens to be a very good suit of armor, wasn't there to block it. This was my first lesson as well – the collapse of the ego feels unnatural and disorienting. It isn't the way we normally move through the world. That's a shame because its collapse isn't to be feared. It opens up a way of connecting with human beings on a much deeper, more profound level.

There were lots of wonderful people who attended Ryan's wake and came back to my house afterward. One was my dear friend Michael. Out of the blue, I heard this small voice inside me say, "You have to ask Michael for a ride on his motorcycle." Well, my rational mind jumped right in and said, "You can't leave. You have a house full of guests here for you." But I knew I had to listen to that still, small voice. It was very compelling. It was the voice of my intuition or my inner being – my higher self. I went and asked Michael to give me that ride on his motorcycle. We rode down to the ocean on his bike. We went over 85 miles an hour, the wind was blowing against my helmet, and the noise level was high – but still, through all of that, I heard that still, small voice again. This time, as it spoke to me, a brand-new, tiny, pinprick hole got created in the black, and the darkness that had been enveloping me, and some light was streaming through that tiny little hole. Also at the same time, the voice said, and I could feel these words being said, "Everything's going to be okay someday." That little hole created in the total darkness was letting hope in. That's an important piece. From that moment on, I knew it was still going to be dreadful. It was going to be devastating. I had a hope that someday, it would get better. Had I not listened to that still, small voice, I wouldn't have received that second gift of hope. Listening to the still, small voice was the second thing I learned in my dark night. And still, every morning I woke up and it was like the worst version of Groundhog Day ever.

Every morning, as soon as I awakened, my first thought was, "Ryan is dead." Day after day, until one day, I got to the point I could say, "Ryan's dead. Now what?" This was me moving into acceptance and pivoting toward what was next for me. It's a necessary step in our evolution through the dark night and into the light of infinite potential. Lesson number 3: Each and every day, I'd focus on that little bit of hope I had, to the best of my ability. More often than not, I was focused on the grief. I was nurturing that hope on a daily basis, and it was growing. The next lesson: We have to nurture whatever hope we have, to make it grow. Because hope is the doorway, the portal to all the good that's in store for you. I realized that this was the worst chapter of my life ever, and I was pretty clear it always would be, but it wasn't my whole book. There were still other chapters to write – and this was not how my story was going to end.

For many years, I had tied my identity to being a banking executive – and I was really grateful to exchange that identity to be Ryan's mommy. Now, after leaving banking and with Ryan dead – I was temporarily in that void. I felt that sense of void in the dark night – that desolate place where I didn't even know who I was anymore. I had to find a new identity. I had to find out who I was – without being executive and without being a mom – and there's grieving around that, and that's the fifth lesson that I learned from the dark night of the soul: You have to create a new identity. When your dark night of the soul hits, and your identity is shattered, it holds within it the seed of a whole new, never-been-experienced identity.

Before my son was born, I loved my adorable little fluffy white dog Molly with all my heart and soul. She was my baby. I didn't think it was possible to love anything anymore than I loved Molly. And then, when Ryan was born, I discovered that there was a whole other level of love – something I didn't know anything about before. So it was with my love for God or Source or a higher power – whatever you want to call – before Ryan's death, I loved God with all my heart and soul and didn't think it was possible to love God any more than I did. Through that opening that was created I came to know a whole deeper, more experiential way of loving – and being in a relationship with God. That brought me to my next lesson, which is that the dark night of the soul has the potential to open you up to a whole new relationship with your higher power. This was an experience that changed my entire life. And now, my work, which is my absolute passion and joy, is supporting people and guiding them through their transformations. The dark night of the soul created such transformation for me. It enabled me to tap into my infinite potential. So Albert Einstein, Thomas Edison, Rudolf Steiner – many, many others – although they refer to it by different names, they all tapped into their infinite potential. We can move into our own unique version of our unprecedented lives. There's a natural inclination to want to avoid feeling what there is to be felt there. That's normal.

Yet it's in those dark places that we don't want to go – that's where there's richness and fertile soil. It's going to require the light of day at a later time – but for it to begin its growth, it starts in darkness. Out of the darkness, something beautiful emerges. And so it is for us: Something beautiful is going to be brought into existence by means of you – the dark night of the soul not only can open you up to your infinite potential, it will bring with it amazing gifts.

So how do you go from the darkness to the light?

Some people have several or many dark nights. It could be anything; your company closes down on you, or you lose your home. The first step, outlined in my gift below, is to make peace with where you are and surrender (which has a very bad rap). Surrender has authentic power. Resistance is a force. You want to completely surrender – when you are able. You want to give up the fight because you cannot access your infinite potential through resistance or fighting. Surrender is a key step in your transformation.

Then you want to find out more. After you make peace – by the way, that doesn't mean that you give your approval to anything that was done to you or that's happened to you. It doesn't. You may have been betrayed or wronged or abandoned or dealt a crappy hand. Whatever the circumstances, this is acceptance and allowing, "This is where I'm at right now. This is the chapter I'm in. It's not my whole book." Then, you want to move into the silence. You want to get present. You want to listen for that still, small voice.

While I have unpacked my story for you, the lessons and the steps are the same no matter your dark night. They're all laid out for you. I recommend finding someone who's been through their own dark night of the soul and has opened up their infinite potential that can guide and help you open up your infinite potential. I had mentors, and I found mentors that could help me – because I wanted to get to the other side of it. There's such richness in all the work I've done. Nothing has let me tap into my infinite potential like the dark night of my soul. It just completely opened me up to new levels of being.

When we're in the present moment, we are the observer. While this concept is not familiar to everyone, however, when you are in the present moment, there isn't the past of what has happened. There isn't the future that looks bleak. There's only right now. That's when you have the opportunity to connect with your higher power, to hear that still, small voice and to reflect. From continuing to go to the present moment, I was able to shift from, "Ryan's dead, Ryan's dead, Ryan's dead," which was very unpleasant as well, in addition to the experience of being on that plane — to "Now what?" It's a pivot. It's a conscious pivot.

One of the things that opened up for me, and it doesn't open up for everyone, is that I can have my own blissful experience and the experiential realization that there is no death; that life is eternal. I heard that. When you get in the present moment, and you're broken open like that, and then you get to experience that.

I don't want the readers to think for a moment that you have to be a guru on a mountaintop to hear the still small voice. I started my transformational work 30 years ago. Before that even, that voice was there. It's there for everybody. It's your intuition. We're born with it. It will try to speak to us. We can recognize it. It's like the voice of someone you know — but it whispers. It will never lay out all the steps that you have to take. It will just simply say, "Go ask Michael for a ride." It won't tell you why. It'll say, "Don't park here." It'll say, "Take a different way home." Yet it won't ever tell you why. You must learn to trust it. I'm telling you that if you think you don't or can't hear it, you do and you can. You simply have not recognized it yet. But it will guide you and lead you to your highest self.

I extend my heart and my love to you, the reader. If you've already gone through a dark night of the soul, you get a hug and my heartfelt love, too. Look at the steps I've outlined. There is gold to be mined in the dark night of the soul. So if you're going through it, look for the gold. And if you've already been through one, then go back and look and see if there's something that you left behind that could benefit you now.

Download Susan's Gift HERE:
http://susanwalsh.com/dark-night-infinite-potential/

SUSAN WALSH BIOGRAPHY

Susan Walsh is a highly sought after and highly recommended transformational coach, speaker and results expert. She is an extraordinary catalyst – leading people from uninspiring lives to Unprecedented Lives. Her expansive depth and breadth of knowledge and application of that knowledge, in the lives of her clients and her own life has won her the admiration and recommendation of world famous industry leaders including: Tony Robbins, Lisa Nicholas, John Assaraf and Mary Morrissey as well as all of her clients.

For 30 years Susan has immersed herself in what she loves: the work of transformation and personal development and she is passionate about helping people create and sustain breakthroughs to new, exciting levels of living. She is a Certified Transformational Coach and licensed to deliver The Avatar Course. This, coupled with her prior leadership experience as a corporate executive, is all expertly combined to have you arrive at a place you once thought was impossible. She will guide you by small steps and quantum leaps to an extraordinary, fulfilling life where you can successfully live your purpose and passion.

Susan is an inspiring speaker who captivates and engages audiences by connecting with them in a powerful way. Susan has shared the stage with luminaries such as John Assaraf and Mary Morrissey, among others. Her brilliant teachings on transformation, mentorship, success principles, universal laws and tapping into our innate unlimited potential, accompanied by her warmth, humor and a rare depth and authenticity all make her a highly sought after speaker.

JULIE WARD

I'D LIKE TO share a little of my story before I share my awakening moment and the steps I took to step into my infinite potential. Early in my entrepreneurial career, I had a consulting practice. I had what I referred to as "a great life." On the surface, it looked great, that is. I had young kids and a great relationship. Everything was wonderful.

Always committed to taking lots of courses, often referring to myself as a personal growth junkie, I was always asking what's next in leadership for me. Where else could I explore? The truth is, I think there was something unsettled in me – something missing. While on the surface, it looked like I had this remarkable life – and I should have felt like everything was awesome – yet it didn't feel that way. I kept looking for what was missing. Part of me was coping and existing, and sometimes I felt desperate. This phase of my life was about trying to answer questions about myself.

So there I was again. I threw myself into one more executive leadership group; my first coaching group. I had done other courses through organizations, but this was a private coaching group by a very powerful leader in the industry. On the first night, he asked everyone, "Why are you here? Why are you here?" And people had different responses,

"Well, I came because I wanted to hone my blah blah blah" or "I wanted to find out about this or that or whatever." Then he comes to me and asks me the same question, "Why are you here?"

At that moment, I swear he sounded like the voice of God because the question came through him and into my heart. It was profound, deep and by no means surface. It took my breath away. It was bigger, so much bigger than, "I'm here to get this x, y, and z." It was disturbing. I think, in the moment, I fumbled and I gave some lip-service x, y, and z answers to why I was there. It wasn't until that night that as I'm driving, I'm asking myself, "Why are you here? What is your life purpose? What are you meant to do that's juicy, that's rich, that's decadent, that's powerful, that's fulfilling?" And it was that night that I hit on the idea of my sweet spot. I'm drilling down, finding myself asking a new question, "What is your sweet spot?" This was my awakening moment.

I knew what it was, my sweet spot. It was intimacy. Not intimacy around sex, but intimacy being able to show up and knowing myself that deeply – and being able to help people that deeply. My stand in the world is about families that work – there's so much suffering out there. I've suffered in my relationships, and I know if I had someone like myself to work with, my suffering would have been less.

It's not about my being arrogant. I simply didn't have the resources I needed. I didn't know where to go to be able to reconcile the anxiety and the angst and the projection of my issues onto my partners and the like. I didn't have those resources to understand what was going on inside of me. It wasn't about them – it was about what I could be responsible for. That's how I landed as a relationship and intimacy coach.

Once I realized this, my first thought was if I am going to do this, how can I be the absolute best of the best at delivering the message. I would be holding other people's lives in my hands. I didn't want to go and get the shoestring certificate. And I realized that I can do this now.

My first step was to dive into researching – and my second step was registering for a coaching program through the Coaching Training Institute.

My awakening was an epiphany. Making that decision was like, "Boom, this is what I'm going to do." I had no clue how it would turn out – it was just stepping into the unknown and on faith.

The next morning, the newspaper arrives, and the front page article is about the up-and-coming profession of coaching," and it had everything I needed to complete my research. It listed the top leaders in the industry, on the front page. So my research was easy. All I had to do is read the article and then go start checking out these different coaching organizations that offered coaching as a training modality.

I already had a lot of other modalities in leadership and self-expression under my belt. But to actually coach, I wanted to have the cream of the crop training – and I ended up with CTI and taking their yearlong intensive certification process.

I started my coaching practice with those attracted to me: career and executive (C-level) women in transition. Transitions either in the relationships or in their life. Very powerful, strong women came into my sphere of influence.

There was another moment in my progression before I landed and came out the door talking about intimacy, my niche. At first, it was executive coaching because I believe we are all mirrors of one another, whether past or current, different forms of ourselves at different times and stages of our life. So women that were attracted to and resonated with me was because they saw themselves in me.

When I was in the corporate environment, very powerful and successful, these are the women that were showing up. When they started doing their inner, the intimate aspect of it, there were similar qualities among them. They were powerhouses, "Go, go, go. Yeah, it's a man's world out there, and I'm right in there, and I'm doing great." It was very high-energy, very assertive – almost to the point of aggression, but not quite. They were tired and exhausted. They spoke from a shameful place within themselves. Their words were about shame like it was some hidden secret that they couldn't share. They'd say, "I used to be fun. I secretly want to get home and put away my laptop and the briefcase for the night. I just want to get down on the floor and play with my kids."

They felt shameful and guilty for wanting these things, as though they couldn't claim that aspect of their identity. Those aspects, these things about wanting to be with children, wanting to be fun, wanting to be engaged in life fully, are feminine qualities, right? At that time I did not yet have clear distinctions about masculine and feminine qualities.

Having that polarized distinction between masculine and feminine was crucial to my being able to pull things apart – so that we could put them back together in a way that works and for the relationship and family.

So my next transition was to start studying practices in sacred sexuality, the concepts and constructs of divine masculine, divine feminine and sexual polarity. Some people may understand that through the world of Tantra. We've done a disserve to Tantra in our western culture as we have overly sexualized it. It seemed to be about "How to get the girl, how to get the guy," thing yet it's not about that at all. It's about sacredness, a special place of being able to have conscious loving, being present and honoring the divine masculine and the feminine in each of us.

My newsletter is filled with guidance and coaching around relationships and intimacy. You may receive it below.

Download Julie's Gift HERE:
www.JulieWard.com

JULIE WARD BIOGRAPHY

Julie Ward is savvy and seasoned at guiding high-achieving women to embody their feminine leadership. She offers deep insight and wisdom on intimacy and relationship in a light-hearted, earthy manner through unique private sessions and group workshops to men, women and couples. Julie's natural ability to form collaborative relationships, coupled with her deep love of family called her to shift her Executive Leadership practice, established in 1996, to Transformational Body-Centered Psychotherapy and Relationship Coaching, Since 2010, her practice is deeply influenced by her world-class sexuality and intimacy teachers, Michaela Boehm and David Deida.

CONCLUSION

THE STORIES YOU have read were transcribed from an online tele-summit. They are written specifically for you to recognize your next awakening and your immediate action steps to keep the new idea alive.

While you may read them in any order, it is important to note that our goal is for you to cease wasting any time being confused by any idea or awakening you have, and get into action right away. Once you do, your next steps will be 'given' to you as you move.

Learning is the 'miracle-grow' for human beings. And we learn because we can be consciously aware that we are learning. It is our unique gift as a species for no other living thing can take an idea which is 'thought energy' and turn it into physical form, another energy.

The only difference between you and Merlin the Magician is that what you want takes time and Merlin 'seemed' to do things overnight. He didn't. It took him days, weeks, months and years, just as it takes you, even though in books and movies we are made to believe that Magic occurs overnight.

If you dreamed of having magical things happen to you as a child and still do today, by embracing the concept that "things are at work even when you haven't yet learned them," you will be delightfully surprised at how our universe makes sure, if we are willing, we will realize our own potential.

ABOUT THE AUTHOR

LESLIE FLOWERS IS a certified speaker, coach and business consultant since 2008, devoting the last ten years of her twenty year personal development career with a burning mission to help women crush the wage gap by 2025, 30 years earlier than predicted, by teaching them to "Ask for what they deserve ... and be paid!"

Living in Northern California in the early 60's, Leslie was part of a semi professional reparatory theater company, went to San Francisco State College, majoring in drama and humanities, danced and played Flamenco guitar, and sang in a folk rock band. In the late 60's, she signed on as stewardess taking troops into and out of Viet Nam from Oakland CA. Her dream? Travel to the Far East and be paid to do it.

Retiring from a 45-year career in Corporate and working 20 years in personal development, in 2008 Leslie began studying and teaching the all time classic *Think and Grow Rich*. Since then she has accrued more than 14,000 hours facilitating seminars and workshops and mastermind studies, using her unique ability to articulate complex concepts in simple, easy to apply, 21st century terms.

In 2014 her book Champion, became an Amazon Best seller in women and business and Leslie refers to it as "the unofficial *Think and*

Grow Rich for Women" as it outlines the high points from the classic, making the concepts more easy to understand and apply.

Subject matter expert in performance, achievement and mastermind, Leslie created Excelerate Experience Events in 2016 to help women learn the skills required to be successful in today's business world.

Her mastermind program, entering its 21st consecutive business quarter, the *8 Essentials of Performance and Achievement* includes a 'train the trainer' program with licensing and certification available to those who wish to use her turnkey mastermind program to help other women grow themselves and their businesses by stepping fearlessly into their unique and infinite potential.

Leslie lives close to her children and four grandchildren and refers to herself as a NanaPreneur and an UberNana, enjoying the magical combination of living a life, FINALLY, by design!